THINGS
THAT MAKE
WHITE PEOPLE
UNCOMFORTABLE

Praise for *Things That Make White People Uncomfortable*

"This book doesn't only explain the roots of Michael Bennett's courage. It will inspire the people who read it to conquer their fears and fight for what's right."
—DR. JOHN CARLOS, 1968 Olympic medalist

"It would be easy for Michael Bennett to remain silent, to play in the NFL and make his mark through accomplishments on the field. Instead Michael has chosen to use his voice and his platform to fight injustice."
—SENATOR BERNIE SANDERS

"This is a brilliant, disturbing, and courageous exploration of race and whiteness in America. Michael Bennett is not only a champion, he's a modern warrior for justice!"
—MICHAEL ERIC DYSON, author of
Tears We Cannot Stop: A Sermon to White America

"Michael Bennett invites us into a vision of justice and liberation that is simply irresistible. This book is pure fire."
—NAOMI KLEIN, author of *No Is Not Enough*

"This is one of the most courageous books on race and racism in America that has ever been written by anyone. It's that good and that important."
—SHAUN KING, columnist for the *Intercept*

THINGS THAT MAKE WHITE PEOPLE UNCOMFORTABLE

Adapted for Young Adults

Michael Bennett

and Dave Zirin

Haymarket Books
Chicago, Illinois

Published in 2019 by
Haymarket Books
P.O. Box 180165
Chicago, IL 60618
773-583-7884
www.haymarketbooks.org
info@haymarketbooks.org

ISBN: 978-1-64259-022-7

Distributed to the trade in the US through Consortium
Book Sales and Distribution (www.cbsd.com) and internationally through Ingram Publisher Services International
(www.ingramcontent.com).

This book was published with the generous support of
Lannan Foundation and Wallace Action Fund.

Special discounts are available for bulk purchases by
organizations and institutions. Please call 773-583-7884 or
email info@haymarketbooks.org for more information.

Cover design by Rachel Cohen.

Printed in Canada by union labor.

Library of Congress Cataloging-in-Publication data is
available.

10 9 8 7 6 5 4 3 2 1

This book is dedicated to my parents, who sacrificed for me year after year, who taught me what it means to be a leader and a man, as I watched them work and give.

To my ancestors, who didn't have a voice but who survived: I'm grateful to stand on their shoulders and never let their spirit die.

To my brothers and sisters, whom I love and for whom I am so thankful.

To my brother Martellus, who has been a guiding star in my life and always believed in me when I didn't believe in myself. Our success has been tied together, and we have a relationship that can't be broken.

To the love of my life, Pele, my biggest blessing, who taught me how to love and how to be vulnerable, I'm thankful for you. This book was powered though your love.

To my daughters, Peyton, Blake, and Ollie: I can't say enough for what you guys have done for me. I love you guys. Thanks for making me become selfless. Everything I do is for you.

Last, to people who don't believe in themselves and are scared to be vulnerable: I hope this book encourages you to stand up for yourselves and your communities.

CONTENTS

We have got to make the white population uncomfortable,
because that is the only way to get their attention.

—Bill Russell

I'm not concerned with your liking or disliking me. . . .
All I ask is that you respect me as a human being.

—Jackie Robinson

AUTHOR'S NOTE

I thought it was important to do a young adult version of the book because at some point in time, we have to be honest with young people about what's happening. We build these fairy tales in life—Santa Claus and the Easter Bunny—and sometimes we're not real with our kids about the world they live in. This book is an opportunity to share some truly valuable reflections from the sports figures they look up to. I always say that as an athlete you constantly get told to sell stuff to kids, but you never really just tell them the truth. We never give them a true, honest reflection of the world and the fact that, together, we can change it: the impact we can have, individually, and as a community, when we collaborate.

It's important to help young kids see athletes beyond the things that they do, to see them for who they are as people. When you ask someone about athletes, the first thing they do is talk about stats—they never talk about them as people or the things they do for the community. This book is an opportunity to see a football player as something other than just an athlete: to see him as a human. It's an opportunity for young people to see it's okay to be vulnerable, to think about how to treat each other. It also shows the strength of what we can do as a whole, as a group, when we put our minds together.

Maybe the title will put people off, but at the end of the day, it's really about what's inside. This book is the true definition of "Don't judge a book by its cover." It's about showing that being an athlete is just one side of a person, and that we all have to pay close attention to who we are, and act accordingly, because history repeats the same discrimination and the same violence and will continue on in this vicious cycle unless we reach and teach young people. I want to help kids to have a voice and to find a way to speak their truth.

FOREWORD

Growing up, we didn't have any superheroes dressed in capes, wearing spandex and a pair of freshly skid-mark-free underwear, who looked like us. The caped heroes weren't saving brown people in their movies, comics, or cartoons. Superman came all the way from Planet Krypton to save white folks. Spider-man has never swung through the hood, hanging from his web to scoop a family in the projects from a burning building just before it collapsed. Batman has never rolled through Section 8 in his Batmobile to save anyone. There's a ton of little Black girls who could've used Wonder Woman and that lasso of hers. Unfortunately, they're still waiting. Shoot, you would've thought that Aquaman had gotten the memo that "Black people can't swim" and came to the hood in the summer to hang out by the pool and save lives. He probably would be more popular these days. But he didn't, and people drowned.

Superheroes don't come to underserved communities. Superheroes aren't on earth to save minorities. Superheroes are here to save white America.

Knowing this, as kids, the superstar athletes became our superheroes. They didn't leap over tall buildings, they leaped from the free throw line. They ran faster than speeding bullets through the finish lines, breaking records. They didn't have superhuman strength to break through walls, but they did break down barriers. They didn't come through the hood in the Batmobile, but they did come through in Bentleys. They came to our communities, unlike the spandex-wearing heroes on our televisions. They brought hope, change, turkeys, educational programs, toys, and wisdom with them. Rather than hearing stories through scripts, we heard stories from our heroes' lips in person. Stories that we could connect to, told by heroes who looked like us.

Superheroes we felt we could be. We bought jerseys instead of capes. Gym shoes instead of the required superhero boots. Headbands instead of masks.

These were our truths.

The guys flying across the screen weren't going to save us; it was up to athletes soaring through the sky and slam-dunking. Athletes became our superheroes, and it was up to them to save us. Protect us. Give us a voice. Muhammad Ali, John Carlos, Colin Kaepernick, Tommie Smith, and Jim Brown, to name a few.

So when an athlete protests the state of the world he's seen by many as an ungrateful dumb jock, lucky to be a millionaire for playing a stupid sport. But when we look at an athlete protesting, what we see is our superhero attempting to save us again. My brother Michael is continuing the battle of the supers before him.

WOW! My brother is a superhero. That's something pretty cool to say out loud. I am proud to know that my brother is one of the supers that the minority youth and communities can trust to fight their fights, give them voices, and do his best to protect them.

I always knew Mike would be a superhero because, for as long as I can remember, he's been my personal hero. Saving me so many times over the thirty years we have spent together. I'm old enough to fight my own battles now, and I've discovered my own superpowers, thanks to him, so I don't mind sharing him with the world now. I mean, who couldn't use their personal superhero?

A couple things you should know about this superhero, if you dare choose him to be yours, as I did for most of my life: He can't fly or hold his breath for extremely long periods of time (although he can swim). He doesn't drive an invisible plane or have x-ray vision. He can't disappear, turn big and green, or shoot spiderwebs from his wrist. Now, I am starting to rethink this whole thing. I mean, what can he do? He's more of a Blankman than Batman.

To be honest, Mike had no choice but to be a superhero, because our dad was the original Mr. Incredible, and the apple doesn't fall far from the tree.

So what is Mike's superpower? It's his unfiltered voice and ability to make people uncomfortable. If you ever sat at a table with Mike, you'd begin to feel uncomfortable before the waiter could deliver the appetizers. I mean, the guy wastes no time. He's the dude you have to warn your guests about before coming over, like, "Hey, my bro Mike is a great guy, but there's no telling what he is going to say. But if you listen, he has a lot of great thought-provoking things to say, in between the jokes about your hair, shoes, or teeth." So guess what? This is your warning. Ain't no telling what he's about to say. Enjoy being uncomfortable!

(*Waiter . . . ?*)

Martellus Bennett
January 2018

INTRODUCTION

In the words of the great Bob Marley:

> *Buffalo Soldier, dreadlock Rasta*
> *There was a Buffalo Soldier in the heart of America*
> *Stolen from Africa, brought to America*
> *Fighting on arrival, fighting for survival*

I think as a kid you hear lyrics, but sometimes the lyrics don't touch your soul. Now I feel them. It's like when you hear your favorite song at a Black barbecue. A track like "Cupid Shuffle" comes on and you hear that beat mid-conversation, you put the potato salad down and drop the ribs. Okay, maybe I'm exaggerating. I would never put the ribs down. But the point stands: music can leave you mesmerized. "Buffalo Soldier" did that for me last year when I went back home to Mother Africa.

It has been four hundred years since my ancestors came to this country in chains and in bondage. This year is that four-century mark from their journey across the Atlantic as human cargo to the Americas: beaten, tortured, raped, and dehumanized. My ancestors: tossed overboard so often, it

1

changed the very water in the Atlantic Ocean; tossed overboard so often that sharks trailed the boats, looking for their next meal. My ancestors were muzzled and caged while being fed through funnels. Their bodies were stacked on top of each other like they were put there by the wish fulfillment center of the Amazon Christmas shipping department. My ancestors: living in fear of the unknown, in fear of what, where, and when death would happen. The only certainty was that it would.

In May, on the shores of Dakar, Senegal, underneath a moon so bright it made the ocean gleam like bling around the neck of your favorite rap artist, tears rolled down my face. You would have thought I won the Super Bowl, but I was so full of emotion it came straight out through my tear ducts. Tears of emotion, or was it rage?

I still don't know. I just know that I was feeling things moving around me, like in *Roots* when Kunta Kinte was raised in the air. I felt like it was a rite of passage, just to feel the weight of the knowledge of what happened—the way my ancestors were torn from their land, separated from their families. I am also thinking about what's been on the news, and seeing families from Mexico and Central America separated from their families at the US border. I know the past isn't always the past. I know it feels like this massive burden, anchoring me to this deck in Senegal: wondering why it's on me to be so young, and yet to feel like I must bring the spirit and memory of my ancestors back home with me.

The anxiety and the pressure to do right by their memory was so bad it felt like pregame jitters. The tears fell faster than I could wipe them away. It was four hundred years of pain and anguish—finally fully understanding just how evil humans can be. It was a realization of what must never happen again. It was me shedding my fears. It was the death of old me and the birth of new me. The new me: someone who would continually challenge society and willingly pay the price of speaking truth to power.

When I heard I was going from Seattle to Philly, it felt like the reality of the business end of this game smacking me across the face. When you love a place so much—the way I loved the city of Seattle and the Seahawks—and give so much to something, you just feel like it's a part of you and it's a part of your being. The city, the team, my teammates, they were all a part of my DNA. I had put so much time into these relationships. My life had become their lives. We had merged together: marriages, deaths, money issues… whatever it was, we faced it all and built this crazy bond like nothing else, and then all of a sudden, the bond is broken. All of a sudden, the very thing that brought us together—the game of football—is what was tearing us apart. Now I wouldn't be with these people anymore, these players and coaches, and the connections would be severed. It had been an emotional labor of love, and now that I would be going to Philadelphia, I asked myself on that beach in Senegal, "Can I do this again? Am I able to give myself in a way that is unselfish, in a way that is almost poetic? Do I have it in me, at age thirty-three, staring at the end of my career, to do it all one more time? Can I put the feelings of others in front of my own feelings?"

I think this is hard for all players when they switch teams—not to know if you'll be able to summon the ability to trust coaches or trust an organization or just be able to give yourself to teammates again. I wondered, "Do I really have that anymore?" That's a big responsibility, the burden of caring for others in such a way that requires true passion. I was also hurt to leave Seattle. As you'll read in this book, I feel that we built a locker room at the Seahawks unlike any other in sports, and it hurt to see the players who made that culture leave because of injury, retirement, or trades. We were cleared out. But as much as it caused me pain, I didn't think it was some kind of conspiracy to eliminate the most controversial players (even though some people were making that kind of noise). I think it was just that they wanted to build a new, younger team and recreate themselves. I understand it and I respect that. Everybody has to have the time to reinvent themselves.

As I sat on that beach in Senegal and thought about the trade, it awakened a drive in me to show that I wasn't a Pro Bowler just because I played with all these dominant players on the Seahawks. I wanted to show that I could change teams and still be a dominant player.

It was a challenge to myself, it was a challenge to my character, it was a challenge to my work ethic, and it was a challenge to my skills. But as I write this now, I know that I did it. I picked myself up off the beach in Senegal, with the souls of my ancestors coursing through my body, and I had a hell of a season in Philadelphia, with nine sacks, as one of the leaders in the league in quarterback hurries and knockdowns.

One reason I was able to experience this rejuvenation has to have been the city of Philadelphia itself. Seattle has a great fan base, and I have nothing but love for Seahawks Nation, but Philly was the first time I ever played in a true sports city. In Philly, it's like pure passion. It's "You suck." Or, if you're a fighter, it's "You're gonna get this! We are with you!" They'll get on the radio to bash you or love you to death. It's crazy. I felt this great connection with the fans in Philly. Going there, I think a lot of people expected I was some kind of jerk because that's how some in the media have chosen to paint me, because I actually speak out on issues and ideas I'm passionate about. But we got to know each other and they heard me speak for myself—and then, most important, they saw that I love football. They saw the love I have for playing this game, and I saw the love they had for us. That love was particularly intense since this team was coming off the Super Bowl. Everybody wanted to re-capture that feeling, spiritually, physically, and emotionally. Philly fans got a true chance to see me, because at the end of the day, they saw how hard I played, regardless of injury. They saw the type of teammate I was and what I did for the organization. The fit was very smooth. Seattle has this nerd fan base, but I feel like Philly's is super blue-collar working class. They are working people who really care about their team. They'll cuss you out and everything, and I loved it.

That's not to say that moving across the country was easy for my wife Pele and our three daughters. Adjustments are never easy. But it was made easier because we chose to live smack in the middle of the Philly, and Pele enjoyed that vibe. Also, Seattle just doesn't have too many Black people living there. Philly is 44 percent Black, and for my kids—raised in Seattle and Hawaii—it was the first time they saw themselves as being normal. They didn't feel singled out in school. No one was asking if they could touch their hair. The music they listened to was also the music their classmates were listening to. It was a gift to live in Philly and see my daughters develop a positive Black consciousness. I'll always be grateful for that.

As for the Eagles, it took some adjustment. There is a whole chapter in this book about the special vibe in the Seahawks locker room. The Philly locker room was very different. In Seattle, we had so many superstars and so much fame that it was like watching a television show sometimes. Iconic people all over the place, like Richard Sherman, Russell Wilson, Kam Chancellor, Earl Thomas, and Bobby Wagner. It was kind of cool in Philly to just to sit back and be a part of something different. But the similarity was that, like in Seattle, there were a lot of people in the Eagles' locker room who were doing a lot of things, socially: Chris Long, Fletcher Cox, and, of course, Malcolm Jenkins.

I liked being in that locker room with Malcolm Jenkins. I think Malcolm gets a lot of crap he doesn't deserve. There is all this friction in the football activist world about what he does versus what other people do, because he secured money from the NFL for social programs, even though Colin Kaepernick is still being blackballed by the league. Some people saw that as a kind of payoff to stop protesting. But I can tell you first hand that Malcolm is truly a guy who cares.

I have so much respect for Malcolm after seeing his activism on a week-to-week basis. He has a lot of heart for people. He really puts himself out there. I saw how he goes into communities and helps. He does it in a really compassionate way—he listens to people and tries to figure out how he can make a difference. It was good to see him up close because people do talk their trash, but I can vouch for him and am proud to say, "I know that guy."

I also talk a great deal in this book about my relationship with my Pro Bowl/Super Bowl–winning brother, Martellus. This past year was strange because Martellus had retired. That means 2018 was the first time in eight years that I wasn't playing in the NFL at the same time as my brother. It was very bizarre because we've done so much together and are so connected in our lives. This past year I would look around the league and go, "Dang, Marty is not here." I felt the difference that, for the first time since when we were kids, we didn't have football in common anymore. But it made me appreciate what did connect us. Our relationship grew this year because I had a chance to really sit back and get to know everything that he wants to do in life, how he was going about it, and how much work he puts into his craft. He's one of the hardest-working people I know, writing books, making apps, working on cartoons, music, and so much more. He works really hard on all his stuff and keeps going and going.

My next year is going to be with the New England Patriots. Again, I'm playing for the defending Super Bowl champs. I have no idea what the mix of my personality with

Bill Belichick's locker room is going to be like, but I cannot wait to find out. I hope you are curious, too. We'll find out together.

My favorite author, Pema Chödrön, wrote, "We think that the point is to pass the test or to overcome the problem, but the truth is that things don't really get solved. They come together and they fall apart. Then they come together again and fall apart again. It's just like that. The healing comes from letting there be room for all of this to happen: room for grief, for relief, for misery, for joy."

The task is on all of us. We must dig deep into our past and face our history head on, like a linebacker coming downhill, nose to nose with a three-hundred-pound offense of lineman on power play on third and one. The world is full of pain, and sometimes it can feel like the only way to be active is to whine on Twitter and Instagram, fighting about which philosophy is right. That's not nearly good enough. That's not nearly worthy of the people who sacrificed for us to be here. We must enlist ourselves in actively fighting for what's right for our children's future. We also cannot letting what happened in 2016 election ever happen again, because the divide is real and only getting worse. It's time to stand up. To paraphrase the great Gil Scott-Heron, the revolution *will* be televised, so as you read this book, reflect on your choice, and choose to be different.

THE SIT-DOWN / ON FEAR

> I couldn't see another "hashtag Sandra Bland,"
> "hashtag Tamir Rice," "hashtag Walter Scott,"
> "hashtag Eric Garner." The list goes on and on and
> on. At what point do we do something about it?
> —**Colin Kaepernick**

It was our first preseason game in 2017. I was still with the Seattle Seahawks at the time. I couldn't even tell you who we were playing because the thoughts in my mind were like cars smashing into each other. I was thinking about American Nazis who had just marched in Charlottesville and the young woman, Heather Heyer, who was killed. I was also thinking about Charleena Lyles, mother of four, pregnant, who called Seattle police for help and they shot her to death. I was thinking about my friend Colin Kaepernick, denied a job in the National Football League because of his protests against racism and police violence that he staged during the national anthem, the stand he took for equality and justice. I was thinking about my mom, a teacher for over twenty years, who taught me to question everything. I was thinking about the gap between what we are taught the flag represents and the experiences of too many people. I was thinking about all of this, and as the anthem started to play, I sat down. There was no way I could stand for the national anthem, and there was no way I would, until I saw this country take steps toward decency.

By not standing, I wanted to honor the founding principles of this country—the freedom of self-expression, liberty, and the equal opportunity to pursue happiness—and challenge us to try to reach those goals. I wanted to use my platform to inspire young people to see us not just as athletes or pitchmen for products, but as changemakers.

It was something I had to do. Charlottesville brought back memories of growing up in Texas and being afraid sometimes even to breathe. It brought tears to my eyes to see people armed to attack somebody because of the color of their skin or their religion.

At this point, I think if you're being silent, you're making a choice and taking a side. As NFL players, we cannot be silent anymore just because we have the ability to hide beneath our helmets. I can't hide behind the shield. I can't hide behind the glamour and glitz of football and fame. The reality is that I'm a Black man in America and I'm going to be a Black man in America long after I'm out of this league. There is too much in this country dragging down the poor, women, and kids, and we can't be hiding behind gated communities, pretending these things are happening somewhere else.

So I sat during the anthem and the hate came in, as sure as night follows day. I'll leave out the worst, but I will say that the fact it made people angry, uncomfortable, and even hateful was proof that I was right to make a stand and take a seat. If I'd protested for the right of men to grow beautiful beards like my own, no one would have cared—and if no one cared, then I would have been wasting everyone's time.

Of all the responses, what bothered me most was when people said I was hurting the military. It got under my skin because I also heard from a ton of veterans who said the opposite: they said, "We wore the uniform precisely so people would have the freedom to protest." It bothered me because my father was in the military. I love my father, but I don't love the hatred I see growing in this country. I love the soldier who, after I started my protest, sent me an American flag from Afghanistan, covered in dust and dirt from thousands of miles away, and said he stood with me. I want to use this platform to reach people, to encourage us to see how unselfish we can be. Just because people don't eat what you eat, just because they're not from where you're from, just because they don't pray to the same god you pray to, just because they don't love who you love doesn't mean they should be treated like they are less than human. I want us to aspire to love one another, in all our difference. To me, sitting during the anthem is not being divisive. My hope is to bring people together. But it's so much easier to put up walls.

I also took a stand for Colin Kaepernick. Colin is one of the best fighters for justice and equality in sports history. I think people assumed the anthem actions would go away because he was out of the NFL, but there's still a fight going on. Racism and social inequality haven't gone away. Just because Colin Kaepernick is not playing doesn't mean the fight is over. Like Fred Hampton, a Black Panther leader from the 1960s, said, "You can jail the revolutionary, but you can't jail the revolution." They can lock Kaepernick out of the league, but more and more players are taking up the cause. If the franchise owners thought that keeping Colin out would silence us, that's just insulting. Guess what? For a pro athlete, being told to shut up and play, shut up and dance, shut up and take the warning pushes us to want to push right back.

It makes some people so angry to see us taking a stand (or taking a knee). I get that they watch football to escape, and they view us as entertainers, here to give them a break from the so-called real world. But we aren't machines. We are human beings, and we aren't paid to stand for an anthem. We are paid to play football—this is our "real world." Maybe some people figure that being a professional athlete means we aren't affected by racism. But if I'm someplace where people don't know me as Michael Bennett, I am a Black man, judged by the color of my skin. I lived through this in August 2017, in Las Vegas, where I was put on the ground, a weapon placed against the back of my head, and a police officer said he was going to "blow [my] f---ing head off." (I'll be talking more about that night later, because, in this case, what happened in Vegas isn't staying in Vegas.)

We have the right to protest, and we, like anyone else, can try to be heard. They also tell us to stick to sports when we speak out on issues. But they don't seem to have a problem when we're making commercials, selling kids sneakers they can't afford or fast food that will hurt their health. I don't see how that is sticking to sports, but somehow that is considered okay. This cartoon by my brother Martellus nails it:

The reaction to all of this went off the charts when Donald Trump gave a speech at a rally in Alabama that attacked us for protesting and went after the NFL for not firing us. He also described any player who took a knee as a "son of a b---h." Well, all right then. No confusing how he feels. He took the flame that Colin had lit and poured gasoline all over it. But Donald Trump never played football and does not understand our brotherhood. I'll go into that later—what the NFL brotherhood is and what it means—but I knew that our brotherhood would come into play. That's why, as soon as I heard what he said—and my phone started blowing up and the fury of my friends was making my ears bleed—I felt really calm, almost like a big, bearded Buddha.

Even though he singled out those of us who protested, I felt like he was taking on the whole NFL, so I never really felt alone. Instead, I felt an incredible sense of positivity. I just thought, "Hey, he's entitled to his opinion. I'm not about to go back and forth with him because that's not what this is about. I don't know who that helps." A lot of players were tweeting and talking volumes of anger. NBA player Chris Paul even dared Trump to say it to our faces (he hasn't). My only public response was that he shouldn't be saying "son of a b---h," no matter what he thinks about us, because, president or not, you don't talk about people's mothers. In a tweet, I wrote, "My mom is a beautiful lady and she has never been a b---h."

But I was also proud. Wow. We got under the skin of the president of the United States. I was grateful. Even though he disagreed with us, he turned it into a worldwide conversation. Maybe he wasn't willing to have a discussion with us about what we were protesting and why it mattered. But his comments did allow for us to go global with the problems of racism in this country. He also brought the NFL family together, activating the brotherhood, as if his comments were some kind of NFL bat signal.

His mistake was taking on the whole NFL. Owners don't like it when you tell them who to hire and fire, and you don't talk about people's moms. He also crossed a line when he said that the game has become "too soft." Everyone in the NFL, from owners to players, knows the toll this game takes on our bodies, and nobody who sees us after games or in the training room would dare say such a thing. In that moment I saw the part of the man that makes me feel pity: he has no ability to walk in other people's shoes, to see the world from another perspective. He doesn't know what it's like to wrench your neck because someone faster and stronger than anyone who played even twenty years ago hits you like a truck. Yes, the rules have changed, but that's because players are so big and fast now. There wouldn't be any of us left if the head-hunting days were still in effect. I heard that part of his speech and just said, "He don't really know. You know?"

Then on Sunday, September 24, 2017: history. It was the first time the national media had covered the anthem actions, and the protests hit every single team. You even had Trump supporters on the pregame shows—like former coach Rex Ryan, who had introduced him at campaign rallies—taking the president to the woodshed. The previous Sunday, nine of us players had protested during the anthem. Now we were talking 180 to 200 people: players, coaches, even owners. It was a league standing together to say that we were not going to be treated like this. More than any issue for which we had knelt before, now the protests were also about self-respect. Josh Norman, the cornerback for Washington, put it the right way, afterward:

> It's not about the flag, man. . . . Nobody is spitting on the flag or disrespecting it. We know you gave your life for it. We know that. And our gratitude to your services is deeply endeared. Understand that. *But* if somebody comes on your front porch and takes a piss, as a man, what are you going to do? Sit there and just watch him pee? Or are you gonna step outside and be like hey, what are you doing sir? You're on private property. You've got to get off, or we'll *make* you get off.

What a day that was. Some raised a fist, some knelt, some linked arms, and some stayed in the locker room while the anthem played, our absence being the strongest possible statement. That's what the Seahawks did, and the team we were playing, the Tennessee Titans, did the same thing. Meanwhile, the woman singing the anthem, a country performer, took a knee. That made two anthem singers that Sunday who took a knee on the last note: a Black man in Detroit and a white woman in Nashville. In a divided country, we were forging unity: the unity of people who think we can do better.

What was so cool about the Titans also staying in the locker room was that it didn't come out of a long conversation with the players on that team. We were all just on the same wavelength and did what we believed in. In that moment, we shared a blessed common direction.

On our team, it wasn't easy to get to that place. The day before the game saw an emotional discussion. Everybody was expressing their feelings, talking about what they'd been through emotionally, physically, and spiritually over the previous twenty-four hours, and some people had different ideas about the protests. Trying to help all of us understand was not easy, and conversations definitely got heated. I can't even say that we truly came together. We talked about all kinds of things we could do, and in the end, we had about 75 percent of the team buying into the locker room plan.

We also issued a statement that I'm very proud of, explaining our reasons. It read:

> As a team we have decided we will not participate in the national anthem. We will not stand for the injustice that

has plagued people of color in this country. Out of love
for our country and in honor of the sacrifices made on our
behalf, we unite to oppose those that would deny our most
basic freedoms. We remain committed in continuing to
work towards freedom and equality for all.

A big group of us worked on the statement. Different people
picked apart and rewrote certain sentences or pointed out
what they wanted changed. There's an old saying, "A horse
by committee is a hippopotamus," but I thought we ended
up with a pretty cool hippopotamus.

One aspect of the experience that was really special was
when our quarterback, Russell Wilson, stepped up, in the
locker room and to reporters, in support of all of us. We've got
some big personalities in this locker room, and up to this point
Russell had never been at the center of it when the political
fires were hot. But he got in front of the team, and I was just
proud to know him. He was emotional and he made clear that
doing nothing wasn't an option. He said to the press, later:

> I was passionate about it because I am really more con-
> cerned about what is next for our future and for our fu-
> ture kids, and what we are going to do with the people
> [who] are going to lead this world someday. I pray for my
> kids every day that when they go to school that racism
> isn't a thing that stops them from going where they want
> to go. It's not just my kids, it's your kids, it's everybody's
> kids, and I think that is really critical. That was on my
> heart, especially.

It meant a lot to the players, but it also meant a lot to "the
12s," the crew of Seahawks fans around the world. Russell is

a superhero to both Black and white communities in the area. He's an icon. His service work is amazing. And for him finally to voice his opinion on behalf of the people who love him but can't afford to go to a game moved us all very much. It's a reminder not to judge someone for not speaking out but to create the space so that when their time comes, they're ready.

As for the games that Sunday, they were a blur. That's how intense the reaction was. Every contest felt overshadowed. It was the first time in this country that sports had ever been like this, with everybody watching to see what we were going to do, not how we were going to play. That's never really happened before. Ever.

It wasn't perfect. There is no doubt that the original message of protesting racism in the criminal justice system, and supporting Colin Kaepernick, got a little lost. How could it not? Yet I think we just have to keep pushing forward. We have to keep going so more people can get involved.

A few weeks later, a committed group of players was present at the annual NFL owners' meeting in New York City. I was proud of what we were able to win: economic support from the league for some of our programs, in particular. But I don't want us to fold so quickly just because the franchise owners chose to go with the carrot instead of the stick. In the meantime I'm going to keep sitting and using the space during the anthem to protest, because there are two parts of how things have gone down that feel wrong to me. The first is when Cowboys owner Jerry Jones said that players "disrespecting the flag . . . won't play. Period." That's crazy to me: saying we'll celebrate freedom by forcing people to stand.

Then he explained that he was "helping" us because we "need consequences" in order to stand up to peer pressure. I'm a thirty-three-year-old man, father of three, and that's the most patronizing thing I've ever heard in my life. If you think about what Jones said, it's treating players like they're not human beings. It sends a terrible message to young people: that your boss doesn't see you as a human being; they see you as a piece of property. We have every right, according to our union and according to the freedoms we are supposed to be honoring, to use that space to do what we like. This game has given us so much, but it also takes so much away: our health, our time with our families. It seems like Jerry Jones is on the hunt for our dignity and our humanity, too.

The second part that sits wrong with me is that I believe central to any conversation about standing for the anthem is making sure Colin Kaepernick has an opportunity to play in the NFL. Before we negotiate anything about whether we sit or whether we stand, we need those doors for Colin to open up, to stop the collusion against him that hasn't really stopped even though he settled with the league. It felt so wrong for us to have the opportunity to be able to speak honestly with our employers but for the guy who started everything not to have a voice or a seat at that table.

Going forward, we know that the owners are driven more by the bottom line, while we have more of a social justice view, so trying to align those is going to be hard. I will say that the best way they can show that they are truly with us is—as of this writing—to sign Kaepernick. He deserves more than just a place on a team—he needs to be on the front lines of what we are doing. Any effort to erase him from this moment needs to be fought.

Some members of the media have been growling like junkyard dogs throughout this whole experience, and fans—outside Seattle—yell things at us now that wouldn't be out of place in the Alabama of the 1950s. But, truly, I've felt chill through the whole thing. I've been studying Martin Luther King Jr. a lot, reading biographies and his speeches, and one of the bits of wisdom I've gained is that hate comes at you when you make any stand. It's the price of trying to be heard. If that's the case, and we accept it, then it's a waste of emotion to react to the negativity. The hate, the rage that people throw at you only has power if you let it affect you. I know that's easier said than done, but I want to enjoy every single day and feel great about the power of this struggle that we're building. Dr. King tried to love life, make time for his family, and keep his humanity intact. Reading his lectures and spiritual teachings is pushing me toward a clearer understanding of what you have to do to find balance.

Reacting to every slight—whether from someone online or even the president—doesn't put you in the right mind to make smart, calculated moves. The week after all this happened, I was doing my regular work with youth at a jail detention center, talking to the kids about what makes a person strong. I asked them, "If I'm sitting in front of a white man and he calls me a 'n----r,' am I a man if I punch him in the face? Or am I a man if I think about my kids, and think about the consequences of what could happen if I did punch him?" For me, that was a moment to acknowledge that I'm a man

if I think about my family first, not if I think about myself first. It's not about the short-term satisfaction of responding to every impulse.

This approach allowed me later to experience true grace—in a lot of situations that I don't think the president expected to create. I felt that grace the week after the big Sunday showdown, when I rolled up to practice in my car and saw people protesting outside our practice facility, waving American flags. I pulled over outside the security gate and got out of my car to talk to them. I'll admit it was a little scary. But I saw them protesting, and I was just like, "Hey. Let's talk." At first they were shocked. I don't think they expected to be talking with players when they showed up to the facility with their flags and signs, but it was cool. We just shared our experiences. We talked about where we disagree, yet how we want the same things, and what the flag means to them. They said I could never understand what they've been through. But they also admitted that they could never understand what I've been through as a Black man in America. I also explained—and it seems I can't repeat this enough—that these protests are not about the military, and they should not believe anyone who says otherwise. They said they understood all that; they just wished we didn't disrespect the flag. I told them we did not disrespect the flag—we're trying to honor what the flag is supposed to represent. And, kind of like an after-school special, we expressed to one another that we could all understand what it means to be human, with a need to protect our families.

Then another woman pulled up. She was bawling her eyes out because she was driving by and saw the protest signs, the flags, and all of us talking with so much emotion. She said she was caught between the old and the new; she loved the Seahawks but didn't want anyone in the military to feel bad. She wanted to respect the military and also support equality. We ended up talking for about twenty or thirty minutes. Nice lady. I am glad she pulled over, for safety reasons alone. (Don't ever sob and drive. That's just dangerous.)

But I was also ready for it. Throughout this experience people have been coming up to me, very emotional, saying, "Thank you." Black and brown people who have felt the sting of inequality; white people who are wrestling with these injustices for the first time, crying as if they are newborn, angry at the world they're seeing for the first time; and vets who have said to me that military people are divided in their opinions as much as anyone else, and they didn't want me to cave to the lies. For me, it's been powerfully emotional and a little bit over the top. Seriously, imagine people coming up to you, weeping, several times a day. It can be exhausting. But I wouldn't trade it for anything. For all the people who say they hate me and want me out of this country—which my family's blood and sweat built from the ground up—there are more people who sympathize with what we are all trying to do, who want to see a better world. I treasure this time because it's like water in a canteen, and in the future, when my throat is dry, I'm going to remember all these people and keep pushing forward, with my eyes on the prize.

The goal is worth the sacrifice. For me, it's always been about pushing people to respect one another in every facet of life. The loss of a human life is the hardest on those left behind. That's the end of everything. There are no more walks in the park. "Black Lives Matter" is saying that all of our lives have value. If a soldier loses his life, it's just as important as young thirteen-year-old Tamir Rice losing his life at the hands of a police officer just because he was playing with a toy gun. We need to celebrate every life and mourn every death because behind every one is a family in pain.

As everything was raging all around me—the president cursing my name, fans yelling slurs—I felt oddly at peace. Martellus said to me, "Bro, you sound like you're sixty years old." But that doesn't mean there wasn't fear. We need to talk about fear, because when you feel that fear, it means it's real.

On Fear

It can be a burden to stand up and speak your truth. You feel disheveled, isolated, like you are holding up the earth and it could all come crashing down. You know it's going to be hard before you start because so many people tell you not to do it, to be quiet, to shut up and play. But it's even harder than they warned you: the anxiety will scratch at your insides like the creature in *Alien*, except it never bursts out of your chest, it just stays there, scratching.

You grow up wanting to be a positive force, to try and change the world for the better, but when the opportunity comes to step up, when it knocks at your door, I can tell you the question changes. It goes from, "Wow, wouldn't it be great to do something like that?" to, "Whoa, do I really want to do something like that? Do I really want to put my family at risk? Do I really want to be judged by people who don't know me or care to understand my motivations, no matter how clear I make them?" It's like the difference between watching *Die Hard*, thinking how cool it would be to take on a building full of terrorists, and doing it in real life, jumping off the roof with a fire hose tied around your waist. You'd be scared, peeing down your leg.

It takes a lot to put everything on the line: your livelihood, your morals, your community, everything. I suspect a lot of people think, from a distance, that it's not that hard to do, like, "Oh, I'd be on the front lines. I'd sit. I'd raise a fist. I'd take a knee." But it's so much easier to talk a big game than to actually do something, because once you are out there representing what you believe, people see the real you. Most everybody in the world wears a mask, and very rarely do people show who they really are. And I've done that. So I'm going to be judged by strangers on the core of who I am, and, yes, that makes me vulnerable and it can even feel terrifying. Nobody wants to lose his job like Kaepernick and risk becoming another former NFL player who ends up broke. But if the price of employment is silence . . . I just can't do it.

As I write this now, I'll tell you, I have a particular kind of fear pressing against my chest. I fear not being heard. That haunts me the most. I fear that people will just see the gesture of sitting during the anthem and not hear my reasons, or they'll accept the fake reasons put out by the media. That's why I'm writing a book, because this isn't about sound bites or tweets or Instagram quotes. This is about trying to push forward with a movement that can benefit all of us. I fear that if people don't hear what I'm trying to say because they don't get it or they don't want to get it, or because they have been indoctrinated to believe that the status quo is as good as it's going to get, then there will never be any kind of change. There will never be equality.

I don't fear losing sponsors or friends or partners in my foundation, although that has already started to happen. When you step out like this, you can tell who your real friends are and who truly cares about you. If there are people in my life who don't believe in justice and equality, it probably means that I shouldn't even be messing with them, and that's fine. I'd rather know than not know.

But please don't get me wrong: I do fear the possibility that someone is crazy enough to do something to me just because I'm taking this step. The fear is less for myself than for what it would do to my three daughters. Every single day I think about that. When I'm playing with them after practice or helping them with a project, I'm living in the moment with them as much as I can. I'm doing it more than ever at this point in my life. I am trying to appreciate every second, because you never know what might happen. In a strange way, it makes me feel more alive.

It wasn't that long ago—1965—when Malcolm X was killed. It wasn't that long ago—1968—when Martin Luther King was killed. It wasn't that long ago—1969—when Chicago Black Panther leader Fred Hampton was killed. Fred Hampton knew that the path he was taking would involve sacrifice, and one of those sacrifices ended up being his own life. And in 2017, this young woman, Heather Heyer, goes out to protest some Nazis, with her whole life in front of her, and she's killed. I'm in no way comparing myself to them. I bring them up just to say that it's no wonder more people haven't stepped up. The fear that your life could be snatched is real. Aaron McGruder, the comic artist who created *The Boondocks*, said that he came up with the character of Huey Freeman, the elementary school militant, so we could have a Black voice they couldn't kill.

I asked the activist Angela Davis, someone who has gotten enough death threats in the last fifty years to wallpaper the Smithsonian Black history museum in DC, how she has dealt with being scared. She wrote me back and said, "Yes! I've experienced that fear, but over time, I've learned to accept it in a way that does not immobilize me. Despite all the death threats, I'm still here. Therefore—as the saying goes—I must also be a witness for those who did not make it."

I truly like that idea of being a witness for those who did not make it. That's very powerful, even sacred.

The Seahawks locker room, when I was still in Seattle, was so supportive, because they know my principles and my convictions. They know I wouldn't be doing this if I didn't have reasons. I think they feel like what I'm saying makes sense in a country where we have Klan marching without hoods. Who can disagree with human rights? Who can disagree with fighting injustice? Who can disagree with fighting inequality? If demonstrating for these things makes you uncomfortable, the question should *not* be "Why are you doing this?" The question needs to be turned around: "Why are *you* not?" We don't all have to agree. Disagreements are fine, even healthy. But when crowds are marching with torches and assault rifles, intimidating people from speaking out, and a woman loses her life, the whole narrative changes.

I told my coach, Pete Carroll, "I feel morally wrong to be silent. I feel like silence right now would be an act of dishonesty to people who look like me and people that look up to me. At this point in time, it just doesn't make sense for me not to do what's right. And I know that this might be hard for you to understand, because it's hard for a white man to understand what it feels like to be Black."

Pete Carroll listened, looked at me, and said, "I can't disagree with you."

He later said to the media, "Michael has really dedicated the last few years of his life to try to understand what's going on around the world. He has traveled everywhere to try and understand people's issues and concerns. It has really captured his heart, and he has really turned his focus to doing good work, and helping people, and doing everything he can for things that he thinks where he can help. I support the heck out of his concerns and his issues and all that."

In an odd, funky way, football has prepared me for this more than probably any sport or other job could, save ones that hold the regular risk of physical danger. When you take the field, you have to go out there with the mentality that any play could be your last, and you have to be at peace with that. You have to not just live in the moment but be in the moment.

There have been times I've felt afraid. Having our first baby I was afraid, because our daughter Peyton was so tiny and fragile, and I worried that turning this precious thing into a grown woman was an overwhelming if not impossible task. I'm having a similar feeling as I write this book. It's the fear of the unknown—I have no idea where this journey will take me.

I also fear how *public* my life is and that it is so easy to find me, because everyone knows where I'm going to be on a Sunday. What are you supposed to do? Are you supposed to just live in fear? Are you supposed to put on a mask and act like nothing is bothering you? Are you supposed to hide behind bodyguards and build more and more walls? That's not a life.

Whether I die tomorrow or in sixty years, if the only things about me that people talk about are the Pro Bowls and the Super Bowl appearances, I will have failed. I want my legacy to be what I did in the community and the positive changes this work might have created in people's lives. I want people to know that I was a man of my word, someone who followed through; someone who didn't just talk it but walked it. Records are made to be broken, but the legacy you leave can't be broken, because it's the truth.

I've left a lot on that field. I don't want my legacy to be a limp or a damaged mind. I'm going to have my say and use this platform while I can. It's a brutal league, but the truth is that as soon as I leave, my platform will shrink.

I have got to speak while I still have the microphone: about the NFL, my life, injustice, organizing, and that special locker room we had in Seattle. Some of the topics in this book may make you uncomfortable. I'm going to talk about white owners and Black players. I'm going to talk about the word "n----r." I'm going to talk about my beautiful, scarred body. It might make you uncomfortable, but a lot of what's in here makes me uncomfortable. It makes me vulnerable. And if I'm uncomfortable, why should it just be me?

I hope this book makes you laugh and makes you think. I hope if it makes you throw it in the garbage, you fish it out five minutes later and keep reading. I hope that whatever you think of this book, in the words of my man Maximus in *Gladiator*, you will be entertained.

ROOTS

The triumph can't be had without the struggle.

—**Wilma Rudolph**

When I was eleven, I lifted a tractor with my bare hands. My grandpa, Alfred Bennett, was underneath, fixing the tractor, and the thing was about to fall on him. I didn't want to see him hurt, so I picked the tractor up and said, "Popo, get out from under there!" He scurried out and, true to the man, got right back to work farming. He didn't miss a beat. My cousins froze and just looked at me. Then one of them shook his head and said, "You strong as hell!"

I was. It was old-school strength, developed from the moment I could stand. I was the oldest son, and both my grandpas were farmers. That meant I worked in the Louisiana fields during the summers, which made my hands tough as leather. My job was picking okra and bell peppers and carrying buckets for whatever pay Popo would throw at me. That's what I did when school wasn't in session: farm chores and, when needed, lifting up a tractor. When it was time to have some fun, we body-slammed each other in the cow pastures, right into the mud, pretending to be the wrestler Stone Cold Steve Austin, while the cows looked at us like we were crazy.

Those buckets also strengthened my hands. I've got hands that can crush walnuts. Maybe that is why I wear the tiniest shoulder pads in the NFL. I've never felt the need to enhance anything. As a kid I loved the story about Paul Bunyan, the all-natural muscle man, and I want to feel my muscles work, not just for strength but for speed and flexibility. I still do the same workout. I still lift rice buckets, pull weights, and make sure I'm not just gym-strong but farm-strong. It's like I'm the Black Rocky, from *Rocky IV*, when he was training on that Russian farm. (Or maybe Rocky is the white me.)

But it was when I lifted that tractor and saw the looks on my cousins' faces that I knew I might have a different path from working in the fields.

Louisiana is the foundation for my life. My town goes back to the 1800s. A lot of my family still lives on a street called Bennett Road—same schools, same community, same church. It's where we settled after we were no longer enslaved people, and where the Bennetts have proudly made not just a home but a community. Like I said, both of my grandpas were farmers and worked in the fields. My Popo Alfred also was—and still is—a Southern Baptist preacher. He can preach with the best of them, as good as any of the television pastors in their three-thousand-dollar suits, but he worked with his hands to build his own church in his backyard and packed it every Sunday. Because the church was next to the house, he once caught us playing Nintendo instead of getting ready for services, so he stopped what he was doing, smashed our Nintendo, and got right back to preparing his sermon. He taught me about the Bible, how to hunt and fish, plant, and work a tractor. (I learned how to body-slam from pro wrestling.) One time he had me slaughter a goat, and I did it wrong. The goat bled out quickly, but I felt terrible to see a living creature die. Popo didn't care. He just said, "Death is death, no matter what. When it dies, it's dead." That has never left me. No matter what it is, when something is gone it's gone, so make your mark.

Making that journey from boy to man might have been easier if we had stayed on Bennett Road, but that was not going to be the case. My father, Michael Sr.—otherwise known as Big Mike—and my birth mother, Caronda, started having kids when my mom was sixteen. I was the second of five and the oldest boy. Martellus was born eighteen months after me. By the time my mom was seventeen, she and my dad had three kids, and then five kids by age twenty-two. My dad and mom married right after they both finished high school. They never really got to be teenagers, just went from being kids to being parents. It wasn't any kind of scandal. In a small Southern town, it's normal for people to get pregnant early and get married. But it also meant tough decisions that affected their lives to this day. My dad had a scholarship to play college football at the University of Louisiana at Lafayette, but he abandoned those dreams to support his growing family and joined the navy. (Yes, my dad was in the navy, so—again—don't speak to me about certain players being "unpatriotic" for taking a knee.)

Joining the navy meant leaving Bennett Road in Louisiana and moving to San Diego when I was six. San Diego is one of the biggest navy towns in the country, and we lived there as a family until I was eight, when my mom and dad decided to go their separate ways. That isn't too unusual, but what was different from most divorced families was the decision they made with us kids. Out of the five children, the two youngest went with my mom; Martellus and I stayed with my dad; and my older sister went back to Louisiana to live with our grandma. The family was split, leaving me with the feeling that somehow my birth mother didn't choose me. As I've grown older, I've realized that marriage is hard: to give up your selfish plans in order to build a life with somebody, and to continue to grow while keeping your family together. It can feel next to impossible. Sometimes people grow apart, and trying to keep the family together at all costs can cause so much damage. As long as all the children end up cared for and loved . . . there is nothing more important.

I often think about their choice to split up and separate the kids—how different everything would have been if we'd stayed together or if we'd been divided up in another way, or if Martellus and I didn't end up moving to Houston with a new mom when I was ten years old.

To be honest, if I'd stayed in Southern California, I might not be writing this at all, because gang violence was all over the place. There'd be drive-bys on the way to school, and stray bullets were a daily part of my young life. My dad kept Tellus and me clear of the worst of it, but there were no real safe spaces.

I remember one time a guy in a gang beat up a girl so badly that a group of her people started looking for him. He was running through the neighborhood, jumping over fences, cutting through yards. Our front door was open because us kids were playing football out front. So he ran through our door and headed straight through our house and out the back. About forty-five minutes later, all these gang kids pulled up in their car. They looked ready to search our house, announcing that they were going to get this guy.

My dad came out, no guns, calm as can be, and said, "Y'all come into this house, there's going to be some problems."

Then our neighbor appeared with a massive shotgun and said, "If y'all move, there's going to be a shootout."

Now everybody tensed up. My dad stood in the middle and told everyone to chill out, that there were kids around. He explained to everyone that this dude who ran through our house was nobody we knew. "We don't know what he did to this girl. This has nothing to do with my home or my family."

The gang kids huddled up, and a couple of them realized that they knew my dad from his work as a volunteer flag football coach for kids around the neighborhood. One of the dudes replied, "Nah, you good, you would never do nothing like that." They slowly backed away and waited around the corner. I don't know what happened next, but I can't imagine it was anything nice.

After that, we moved to Texas. You know it's bad where you're living when you're worried about guns and see Texas as a safe alternative. But we really moved because my dad met the woman I would learn to call my mom. In Louisiana for my Uncle Earl's funeral, my dad met Miss Pennie, was struck by lightning where he stood, and just said, "We're moving."

I think about what my life would be if I'd never had the blessing of Miss Pennie, my new mom, a Grambling State University graduate and junior high school teacher, a woman who taught me to stand up for myself. Miss Pennie's entrance into our family was a defining moment of my life. She was somebody who would not let us be "normal," who said that no matter what the world tried to beat into our heads, we could be extraordinary. When I got in trouble, my punishment from her wasn't spankings or sitting in a corner. It was reading encyclopedias. At first I hated it, but I learned to love this "punishment" and would get in trouble just to have some quiet space to learn about the world. Later, I read that studying encyclopedias was what Malcolm X did in prison, and it blew my mind.

Miss Pennie has been there for every important moment of my life. Everything I've learned, I can see now, came from her. How to be the kind of father who can raise daughters. How to love. How to understand this world. I see a lot of kids ask, "Why?" As in "Why are we here? Why is there war? Why are people hungry?" And they get a spanking for asking too many questions. Miss Pennie demanded that we ask "why," and believe me, I took her up on that. I wanted to know why there was hate in the world, why my school wasn't teaching me about our history, and why it felt like, from the schoolyard to the candy store, white kids were treated differently from Black kids.

When I asked her why, she would answer, "I know what it's like out there, and I'll teach you the truth so you understand. But I'm also going to teach you how to survive." She told us we weren't allowed to wear braids or saggy pants. This was not because she thought they looked bad or "ghetto" but because she knew what could happen if we were judged to be somebody we weren't. Miss Pennie was always in my business, scared of what society would have in store for me, a young Black man, if I wasn't on alert, reminding me that racism was real and I'd have to work twice as hard for anything I wanted.

Before Trayvon Martin's murder brought it into some white people's consciousness, Black families have always known, as my mom knew, that if I looked like I was in the wrong neighborhood, or if there were a case of mistaken identity, I could be put down for the crime of walking while Black. I was always reminded that being Black was dangerous, that people would see my skin as a weapon, a threat. But my mom's lessons didn't sink in until I was twelve years old, when a man named James Byrd was murdered in Jasper, Texas, lynched and dragged behind a truck. It brought the history that I was learning to life: the beating and lynching of fourteen-year-old Emmett Till in 1955 and his mother's insistence on an open casket so the world could see what they did to her baby. Mamie Till was also a teacher, like Miss Pennie, and I saw myself in Emmett Till's disfigured face, and I saw my community through the eyes of James Byrd, dragged by the neck from a chain, and I cried until it hurt.

The lynching of James Byrd happened just a hundred miles from my house, and it felt like it happened a hundred yards away. A mental line was drawn in the sand for me, and I don't think I was ever the same again. I saw Black leaders running around, asking for justice again, for another tragedy of a slain Black man. It felt like nothing had changed from Emmett Till's day. It felt like we were being hunted and trophied, to be mounted on someone's wall. I have never admitted this before, but I was scared to walk home at night by myself out of fear that I could be next. For a long while, every time a pickup truck rumbled around the corner, my breath caught in my chest. This was Texas, so pickups were everywhere, which meant that for a while my heart just raced nonstop.

I wasn't the only one in the Bennett household on edge. I remember the time Martellus decided he was going to get lost for the whole day—normal kid stuff—but he didn't tell anybody, and my father went searching for him, guns cocked, loaded, thinking that the worst could've happened to his young Black child.

It made us feel threatened. But it also held a poisonous message that being Black was inferior, that somehow we deserved to be hunted and killed. In Louisiana and Texas, we'd see stories on television of shootings, deaths, Klan marches. In school, we never learned how Black people built this country. We built America, for free, but in class our contributions were invisible, at best there to entertain, or the same lesson about George Washington Carver—as if we were slaves, invented peanut butter, and became entertainers, and that's our entire story. We built the White House. We built the Capitol

Building. We built the Light of Freedom on top of the Capitol Building. That's this country. The Light of Freedom, built by slaves.

Being born Black is a preexisting condition in this society, with a kind of stress that you can't understand without living in our skin. It's not just the fear that you'll be the next James Byrd or Trayvon Martin or Sandra Bland. It's hearing in school about America being the "land of the free" and having to speak up to remind my teacher of slavery, and seeing all the faces change expression, from getting red with anger to others rolling their eyes, with looks of relief on the faces of people who had been thinking the same thing.

I've tried to tell people in Seattle—and I love Seattle— that, yes, Seattle has its problems, but there are parts of this country that are a lot worse when it comes to these issues. Of course there's racism in Seattle. But in Texas, it's right in your face. You're hearing about people getting hanged. You're seeing the KKK. There are Confederate monuments to people who owned your great-grandparents that you have to walk by every day. Until you've lived in that area, you just don't know. Some of the stories my grandfather told me, even what my dad told me, would melt your brain. You grow up in the South, there are people who don't want you alive! They don't want you to have books. They don't want you to even have a chance. I grew up in Texas, and there was a Red Dragon, a KKK leader, right there. This man is walking around, people know him, they say "Hi" to him at the truck stop, and he's full of hate, plotting your death.

But it's more than the fear. My family had been in Louisiana since the late 1700s, but after slavery they didn't have access to bank loans; they weren't able to own anything in their community other than the church my Popo built with his bare hands. We built our own community on Bennett Road. But we had no ownership. Seeing this with my own eyes was a crash course for my experiences in the NFL. That's why I talk all the time about the lack of Black ownership in pro football and why it's so important for us to own and not be owned. There is no self-determination without control, and there is no control without ownership, whether it's your house, your car, or an NFL team.

I only have the tools to navigate both that past and my present because my parents taught us history, including what we had to overcome as a people. Malcolm X once said, "Of all our studies, history is best qualified to reward our research. And when you see that you've got problems, all you have to do is examine the historic method used all over the world by others who have problems similar to yours. And once you see how they got theirs straight, then you know how you can get yours straight." I don't think he ever said anything truer.

Way too often, as athletes, we get some money, get some fame, and become so focused on "the life" that we forget we are still Black men living in this society. It's so easy to lose our sense of self, to just float away on the cheers and forget who we are, who came before us, and how they bled. That mindfulness came from the people who raised me. As I got older, I wanted to follow in the footsteps of the people I grew up reading about in those encyclopedias. I wanted to be a person who made an impact with my mind more than I wanted to grow up and be Charles Haley or my friend the late Cortez Kennedy.

Growing up in Houston also helped me understand this world and my place in it. Living there was an education. You'd see so many diverse cultures and run into so many different types of people that you couldn't help but think about the world outside of H-Town. People don't realize that Houston takes in more refugees than any city in the United States. If Houston were a country, it would rank as the fourth-largest refugee population on earth. Look at the ways people pitched in to save one another after Hurricane Harvey, setting out on boats, pulling people from cars, opening up their mosques, synagogues, and storefront churches. That's Houston, and that was my community growing up.

Our house was where the kids went. We were "the house." Everybody knew where we lived, and they were like, "Let's go to the house." There was always basketball going on and the sounds of kids having fun. Big Mike was the dad for the kids who didn't have dads, or who were in home situations that felt unsafe. They knew they would be all right in "the house."

As for football, I didn't even realize I was "college-scholarship-good" at it until high school. I played because it was something to do. I liked doing science projects, and I also liked football. It was just another pursuit on the list of my interests. I never thought I was going to the NFL. I never believed, "This is exactly what I want to do. This is the dream." But when you're big and Black, the grown-ups push you to play sports. They take an interest that is hard to ignore or resist. Also, when you're big and Black, your peers challenge you all the time to scuffle. They challenge your manhood, as if fighting makes you a man. I never liked to fight, but I really didn't have a choice, because I was Martellus's big brother. Martellus occasionally would start the fights, but I always had to end them. People knew that if they fought one of us, they would have to fight both of us, which really meant that if someone tried to fight Martellus, they would be fighting me. Back-to-back fighting: the big Bennett boys, swatting people down like flies. That was just life. Everybody wanted to test us, every single day. My grandpa said, "Y'all need to stop fighting at that schoolhouse!"

In San Diego, we were "country" to the West Side kids, but in the summers, as soon as we were back in Louisiana, we were "city kids." In Houston we were "the Bennett boys," but no matter how people saw us, we were joined at the hip, two peas in a pod. Growing up, we spent so much time side by side that people thought we were twins. We had the same friends and took part in the same activities. We also shared a bed. I spent my childhood sleeping foot to head with that man. The house had three bedrooms, but my father wanted to have a guest room, so we shared a bedroom. Before we had to split a mattress we had bunk beds, but Tellus got bigger and heavier, growing up to six feet six and 270 pounds, and he was on the top bunk—until it collapsed. I'm still mad about that.

We both went to Texas A&M, so it wasn't until we got to the NFL that we lived in different places and walked our own paths. Before that, we were always on the same team, whether it was football, basketball, or even dodgeball. There wasn't a PE teacher in the state of Texas who was going to split up the Bennett brothers. Even now, when we play against each other, I say I only tackle him enough to get him down. He's got a daughter, and I'm not trying to have to raise her. To this day, he tells me that he looks up to me because of the decisions I make, that he believes in me and I'm his role model. But the craziest part—and maybe he won't even realize it until he reads this—is that, as much as he looks up to me, I look up to him. His creativity, the way he dreams, and his fearlessness about expressing himself. He's my role model, too.

But it's my dad who was, is, and always will be the most important figure in my life. In my mind he's a superhero, but he's also the real-life person who sacrificed for me to be who I am, never missing a game, always being there and doing what he needed to do. He was my football coach most of the time, but more than football, it was his approach to competition and manhood that made the greatest impact.

Once, after a game, the father of one of my friends yelled at another dad, "My son would beat your son up!"

The other dad yelled back, "No, my son would kick your son's behind."

They turned to my dad. "What about your son?"

And my dad just said, "No, no, we're not going to do that. He's going to walk away and live to fight another day." One of the kids pushed forward by his father like a mini-gladiator ended up, years later, getting shot and needing a wheelchair.

My father kept us off the attitude that gets a lot of people in trouble: when, as Dave Chappelle put it, "keeping it real goes wrong." People try to put up a false front, and it ends up coming back to bite them in the ass. My dad would point out our friends who had been shot or lost loved ones to violence and make clear that he didn't want it to happen to us.

When we moved to Houston, my dad found a decent desk job at a company called Enron. Enron went out of business in 2001 because of illegal actions by their leadership. I was fifteen, and we were one of the many families of Enron employees who suffered because of the executives' criminal love of money. We had to move houses and switch schools, and everything got super tight as my dad looked for work. When I speak out on justice issues, I feel like I'm also speaking for everyone hurt by Enron. Corporate greed destroyed the lives of families. None of the company higher-ups asked themselves, "How much is enough?" Or, "Shouldn't we care more about our employees than cheating people to increase our bottom line?" This is why I've never, ever, from day one, trusted the NFL fully, because I know that the bottom line is always the business. When people want the NFL to "lead" on issues like violence against women, or racism, or even head injuries, I roll my eyes. The NFL is just another corporation, and they'll do what they have to do. Asking them to lead on social issues sometimes seems like asking a dog to meow.

I learned early on that I couldn't count on kindly corporations or my teachers to show me morality or teach me my history, but I knew I could rely on my family—and also learned how quickly it could all disappear. I relearn that lesson every time I see myself with no shirt on. In the mirror, I've got my muscles all laid out and proportioned, and I look like what I am: an NFL player in prime shape. But then I've got a scar that runs across my stomach, just below my belly button, about as big and jagged as anything you can imagine. It looks like I escaped from the basement of those *Saw* movies.

The scar didn't come from anything so dramatic, but it was just as deadly. I was ten years old, and my appendix burst. It almost killed me. I was getting ready for school and said to my mom, "I don't feel so good."

My mom, the teacher, cared about education above all else, so she said, "You're going to school, no matter what. You're going to school like it's Walgreens, 24/7!"

I remember protesting, "But my stomach really doesn't feel right." She sent me off anyway. When I got to my classroom, I started throwing up like I was trying to empty my entire body onto the floor. It started with breakfast but then it was green liquid, like I was trying to vomit my stomach lining. I remember thinking, "I'm throwing up poison."

The teacher sent me home, and my mom said to my dad, "Let's just take him to the emergency room." At the hospital, the doctor rushed me into surgery because my appendix had ruptured. That's why I was throwing up so much: all the toxic fluid in my body needed to get out. I had surgery to remove the ruptured appendix, and they thought I was fixed. But I ended up having to go back two weeks later because I wasn't getting better. That's when they had to slice my whole belly open and clean out the infection.

I stayed in the hospital for a couple weeks, and that changed me. My bed was next to kids with burns all over their bodies and other kinds of life-changing injuries. I remember one kid who had been saved from a fire, and he had no skin on his face. I still see that when I close my eyes.

When they finally let me go home, I had a hole in my stomach that needed to be treated. My mom had to put gauze inside the incision to soak up the fluids. For days I had to stay still, and my mom and my dad never left my side. They felt guilty that they'd ignored the symptoms to make sure I wasn't faking to miss school. Now, as a parent, I also understand their panic. There is no fear like worrying about your child. I'd rather go through a dozen ruptured organs and be laid up in bed for months than be in my parents' place beside a hospital bed, looking at my child with a big hole in his stomach. I remember so clearly their love and devotion during those days.

But I didn't know how deeply it had affected Martellus until years later. ESPN did an episode of the show *E:60* on the Bennett brothers, and my appendix rupture came up. Martellus talked about seeing me in the hospital and just started crying on camera, bending down, sobbing. I was as shocked as the camera people. I didn't know what to do, so I just put my hand on his back and let him go. Growing up, I had always seen this story first through my own eyes—my fear, my pain— and then through the anxiety of my mom and dad. I didn't know how much baggage from that experience my brother had been carrying.

Now I stare in the mirror and look at this scar. It's wide, long, jagged, and ugly. It's also a tribute to what I've been through: a reminder that I could so easily not be here. It reminds me that life can be over in an instant, so live every single day. People look at me and think, "Oh, he's so happy, he's always laughing. He's so carefree." Why would I ever sweat the small stuff? I almost died. I'm alive, so to heck with every single thing that you think I should or shouldn't be. I love looking at the scar. I hate that I had to feel that pain, but I love the lessons it taught and the way it still motivates me. Years ago, I got a tattoo of Frankenstein on my leg. Underneath it reads: "Near death experience. Keep on rising."

After I healed up I got back on the football field. Martellus and I both played on the defensive line and put other teams through hell. Martellus was a prodigy, starring in both basketball and football, something unheard of in Houston's Alief School District. I wasn't the athletic freak that Martellus was, but I held my own. Also, through someone on the football team, I met a girl. I was sixteen and she must've been fifteen. I thought, "This is the most beautiful girl I've ever seen." One day there was an open seat next to me on the school bus. She sat down and I couldn't believe it. Her name was Pele Partsch. She and her family were like no one I had ever met: traveling musicians from Hawaii, all in the same band, like a Polynesian Partridge Family. Now they're my in-laws, and Pele and I have been together ever since.

She gave me confidence to push forward with football. After high school, I was supposed to play at Louisiana Tech, but they messed up my paperwork, which gave me a semester to try to land somewhere else. During those months out of school, I sent my game tape to everybody I could think of. I packaged it up and sent it to top football programs. Then I'd call the college coaching staffs, pretending to be a high school coach, saying, "I've got this kid named Michael Bennett. He's got the goods! You guys should check him out. I sent you his highlight tape." That's how I ended up getting a ton of scholarship offers: I realized the recruiters usually didn't watch the full game film—they just heard about a guy and then watched his tapes.

Texas A&M was one of the schools that offered me a scholarship. That's also why my brother ended up at Texas A&M; he was originally going to go to LSU. But now it was all set. The Bennett boys were going to drive two hours from Houston to College Station to attend Texas A&M, but the real education, the real higher learning, would not be going down in the classroom.

THE NCAA WILL GIVE YOU PTSD

> For those of you who think the life of a college ath-
> lete is all glitter and glamour, you couldn't be more
> wrong. . . . But just as with every injustice, wrongs
> don't get righted unless we keep raising our voices
> again and again.
>
> —**Kareem Abdul-Jabbar**

There was a player on Tampa Bay in 2010, when I was there,
a defensive lineman named Brian Price. He was a star at
UCLA, a second-round draft pick. The NFL didn't work out
for him, and Brian was out of the league after twenty games.
In the spring of 2017, Brian was in an auto parts store in Yp-
silanti, Michigan. The video of what happened next is crazy.
He was "acting erratically," so the store managers called the
police. When they showed up, Brian ran as fast as he could
at the glass doors and burst through them, as if the shatter-
ing glass were a left guard trying to get between him and a

49

quarterback. Afterward, he said he couldn't remember what happened and that "mentally, some days I struggle a lot." His wife, Candice, believes his problems are signs of CTE (chronic traumatic encephalopathy—where the brain just starts to fall apart because of repeated hits), and it affects them every day of their lives. Brian is twenty-nine years old.

Remember, Brian played just twenty games in the NFL. So before I say anything about the NCAA, and all the many—many—ways I think it does young people wrong, we need to speak about the price we pay for these dreams. We need to recall what the poet Langston Hughes wrote about "a dream deferred," in terms of trying to have an NFL career and failing—which happens to the 99 percent of college players who don't make it. We need to talk about how this can result in pain, depression, brain injury, and a lifetime of hurt. It's a dream dried up, like a raisin in the sun. And sometimes that dream explodes.

Too many of my high school and college teammates have ended up with what can only be described as PTSD, post-traumatic stress disorder. People might say, "PTSD, that's a crazy term to use for somebody who plays a sport and doesn't make the NFL." But for those top high school players, this sport is their identity, their culture, and their personhood. In college there is no preparation for what will happen to you, how it will feel when you're done, when you don't make the NFL or are just hanging on by a thread. Then the pain hits you like a truck.

I've seen what we should recognize as PTSD in a lot of players. Recently, I was talking to some of my friends now out of the game, and the discussions were about depression;

about feeling like they've let down their families; about a loss of identity; about fears of CTE; about wanting to see a therapist but being ashamed; and, most of all, about how they wish they'd gone into this sport with their eyes wide open. One of my friends said, "Man, I went to a psychologist because I couldn't figure out why I was so depressed, because this word, *depression*, is never said in a locker room. Your coaches never warn you that could happen. You never hear it." His therapist was the one who suggested he had a form of PTSD, and now I can't get that out of my head. I thought PTSD was something that soldiers got in wars, but I learned that it can result from any trauma or pain—not just mental or emotional pain, but as a reaction to physical pain. In football and boxing and MMA—and think about Brian Price when I say this—you develop what could be described as pain addiction. In college you are in this really intense environment, with a regular amount of high-impact physical pain, and then, if you don't make the pros, that kind of physical expression just disappears. One of my friends, who just retired from the NFL, told me he's been having violent outbursts. Not in the sense of hurting people, but he'll be enraged for no reason and doesn't know why it's happening, which is scarier than knowing. He wonders if it's CTE, because his college had no concussion tests, or if he has a pain addiction, or if he is just lost. He just doesn't know. It reminds me of a story I once heard, about a former player whose wife found him running again and again into the garage door because he missed the pain.

I think PTSD in players also results from a loss of identity. Little by little we conform to what our coach wants, what the program wants, what the academic advisor wants us to study so we stay on the field, and bit by bit, chip by chip, we lose the foundation of who we are. We get stuck in a character, and there is no way out. I've been talking to players who want to tell their stories as a warning to parents, a public service announcement so parents don't put their kids through the football pipeline. The problem is that parents have sacrificed so much and put in so much energy to get their kids to the NCAA level that the prospect of not making it becomes unthinkable.

A friend said to me, "Bro, I would just cry sometimes." I know this person as a tough defensive lineman, and he was in tears. In football, it's rare to really know what the other dudes are going through, because you're friends but nobody wants to be seen as an emotional wreck. I felt so sad, and all I could say was, "I never knew." We talked and realized that it's not just a problem with college football; it starts when we're young, when our parents push us in sports but don't let us grow as individuals. We're just walking around for years with no idea who we are. The same friend told me, "I'm thirty-two years old, bro, and I don't know what I like to eat."

If all you've known is this violent sport, you don't know how to shut it off—because you don't know what it is that needs to be shut off. It could be related to CTE, or depression, or just having a massive hole in your life because you thought you had one future but it's not there anymore. It's PTSD. It's people stuck in an identity that no longer exists. They don't know how to love themselves because they don't know who they are.

Fans of college sports need to know this. I hear people say, "I'm an Aggie!" or "I'm a Georgia Bulldog." Fine, but are you still a Bulldog when it comes to the lives of the people under the helmet? Are you a Bulldog when the teenagers you cheered for don't make it in the pros? When they're running through glass just to feel alive?

I'm sure that some fans care, but I know that the NCAA does not. We all know it. Ask most NFL and NBA players and they'll tell you with the cameras off that the NCAA is a gangster operation, a shakedown, and a system that works for everyone except for the so-called student-athletes. The main revenue-producing college sports are football and basketball. The main sports in this country built around Black Americans are football and basketball. The only revenue-producing sports in which you are not paid before you get to the top leagues are college football and basketball. This is not a wild coincidence. We tend to come from communities that are the least empowered, the most desperate for opportunity, so we get the worst end of the stick. It's a bad system that continues because we're too desperate for that chance at the brass ring—the pros—to organize and say no.

Don't let anyone tell you that we get an education, that we're "student-athletes." As others have said, you are an athlete-student more than you are a student-athlete. It's always athlete first, classes last. Let's talk about what a typical day is like when you're playing Division I, Power Conference NCAA football. You wake up at 5:30 a.m. to get in your morning workout. Then you eat as much as your stomach will hold because food access is restricted and money is tight, so you eat when you can and hope it keeps you filled up for the day. That means protein and starches, but a lot of players go the junk food route because it's cheap and vending-machine-ready.

You go to your classes. You make sure you're on time or you'll be doing extra running, something a regular student wouldn't worry about. Then you go to lunch and load up again. After lunch you go to practice, then when practice is done, it's back to study hall. Usually there is also an evening class, because you've designed your class schedule not around what you want to study but around practice and games. It's a ten-hour day, and of course it affects what classes you can take and what you might want to explore intellectually.

I'd challenge anybody to do the equivalent of what we are asked to do and then be fine with not getting paid: dedicate their body, put in ten-hour days, travel, and still stay "NCAA compliant" by handing in the necessary classwork while not taking as much as a free lunch. We do it to generate funds for the athletic department and billions of dollars for conferences and cable networks. We are there to get other people paid and to try to take advantage of that small shot at the NFL. We are there for the dream to earn in the future, not to learn in the present.

My interest was in sociology, yet I ended up studying something a little bit different at Texas A&M: farming. Yes, farming. After growing up in Louisiana, after all those days of picking okra and bell peppers and body-slamming cousins among the cows, I made it to college and ended up back where

I started. They called it agricultural science, but make no mistake, it was farming. It was easy for me, like someone from Mexico taking Intro to Spanish.

I tried to stick with sociology. I wanted to study human beings and understand how they affect and are affected by their environment, but picking up a full sociology course load and playing football felt about as realistic as trying to sack a quarterback while wearing my daughter's ballet slippers. Not even slippers in my size, but *her* slippers. It wasn't just the classwork. As a Black football player, I wasn't necessarily made to feel welcome in the academic world.

During an introductory class, the professor lectured, "The Holocaust is the biggest massacre in the history of the world."

No one said anything, so I spoke up and said, "I respectfully disagree with you. The Holocaust was awful, but there was this thing called Manifest Destiny that justified the slavery of African people, the slaughter of the Native Americans, the killings of Chinese workers. If we called Manifest Destiny 'the American Holocaust,' I bet we'd look at it a much different way."

She answered, "No, no, no!"

But some people in class started clapping. That just got me going even more. I said, "If you look at what happened to the Native Americans, the Trail of Tears, you will cry yourself."

She responded, "That's not true. That was part of making America. It was for the greater good."

So I asked, "Greater good for who? What's the difference?" When she didn't answer, I left. The class was clapping.

I'm still not sure if that clapping was for what I said or because I was leaving. That applause had an edge.

While some of my professors made it clear that I was a football jock they didn't want in their classes, I also believe my coaches did not want me studying the kinds of issues I wanted to explore. They wanted us in classes like farming, classes that would make sure we could stay eligible and get everyone paid.

I clashed with my coaches because they kept telling us, like a broken record, that we needed to be "professional." This bothered me because I thought we were supposed to be "amateurs" and "student athletes," but here they were, telling us to be "professional." I'm a Bennett, so I had questions. I asked them how they defined "professional." They said it meant how we dressed, how we listened, and how we weren't supposed to talk back. In other words, they answered my question, "What do you mean by 'professional'?" with "Being a professional means shutting up, not challenging our authority, and not asking any more questions." It meant we were under their control.

We didn't realize how few of us would make the NFL. We didn't realize how few of us would get our degrees. We didn't realize how little help we'd receive if we were injured. Above all, we never thought or talked about how we could organize ourselves. When we debated the problems of our situation, we'd conclude, "Well, when we make it to the NFL, all of this will seem like a small price to pay." That's how most players in college think, and that's why we get so many stories of the "student-athlete who couldn't make it." There are so many of these individual stories, you wonder when they will finally admit that maybe the system doesn't work. Part of the problem is that the system *does* work for coaches, athletic directors, and administrators. It doesn't work for us, the powerless teenagers getting beat up for free. I had teammates who got injured, needed multiple surgeries over years, and got stuck with the medical bills. Maybe those of us on athletic scholarships don't have to take out loans and have debt, but the debt piles up in other ways. When you are paying for physical therapy out of pocket at age twenty-eight, with no health insurance, or when you can't find work because of a bad back at twenty-five, you know debt.

The ways we were being done dirty were even more obvious at Texas A&M because our coach, Dennis Franchione, was involved in a scandal. He ran a side operation, a $1,200-per-subscription fan-letter service called "VIP Connection." It included injury reports, recruitment information, and private critiques of players. A lot of guys were surprised when it was revealed he was running this kind of game, and that's when it clicked for many of us that college football was both a hustle and a big business. We looked at that "VIP Connection" newsletter, and meanwhile, they were feeding us peanuts. For real. Peanuts. I said, "You got a billion-dollar cable deal and a $1,200-per newsletter . . . Can we get some steaks, please?"

Only now that college is over do we meet up and say, "Hey! We didn't get paid! We built entire stadiums and have nothing to show for it!" All these jerseys being sold with our name and number on the back, all the autographs we signed for auctions and big-money boosters, all this cable money being made, and we didn't get any of the benefits. We didn't realize that you could be a straight-A student but lose your athletic scholarship at any time if you didn't fit into a coach's new scheme. Nothing matters except whether you fit in with the team. A coach will sit in your living room when you're in high school and say to your parents, "We'll take care of your son like he is part of our family, as a university, and we are going to make sure it happens for him. On my honor, he's going to be something great," but it's all a line to keep the train moving.

The largest culture shock was being Black in this atmosphere. We had white coaches, and they wanted the Black players to be just like them. They would tell us to wear our pants or shoes a certain way; this is what it meant to "be a man." They thought our path to manhood was to be found in skinny jeans and a tucked-in shirt. (Although Migos has all kinds of young players dressing like that by choice. Go figure.) But they never understood or tried to understand us. This struck me as a recipe for our continually being misunderstood, misguided, and misjudged, ingredients for disaster and rebellion, or at the very least for stress and self-destruction and the creation of the very PTSD that afflicts players when it's all over.

For all that we faced, we never realized how much power we had. If we had ever decided to go on strike, we could have gotten a new coach, a new university president; shoot, in Texas, we could've gotten a new governor. The Aggies are the identity of an entire part of the state, at the heart of the economic and social life of both the school and the community. We were both powerless and powerful. In 2015, when Missouri players—Black and white—went on strike against racism on campus, the university president was gone as soon as it looked like the school would have to forfeit a million-dollar game check. People were shocked, but I got it right away. We have this power at every school. The only obstacle is our own fear. If I had it to do over, I would have tried to flex that power.

I don't have all the answers, but if I were back in school with my current thirty-three-year-old brain, I'd try to organize players to come together to fight for a list of demands. These would include each player getting a certain amount of money per year, say, $50,000, set up in some type of retirement savings or money market account so they could learn to conservatively manage their money. At the end of their college career, they could have $200,000, plus interest, in a savings account, which they'd be required to keep investing until they were thirty-five or forty years old, so it would continue to grow. That kind of system would also be an incentive for players to stay and get their degrees. Only the best would leave before four years. And please don't tell me that there is no money in the system for this, not when ESPN is making six-billion-dollar television deals to broadcast college football, and Jim Delany, commissioner of the Big Ten, got a twenty-million-dollar bonus in 2017. It's not just Jim Delany, although that story is particularly gross. Athletic directors have gotten raises of 30 percent over the past five years. Don't tell me there's not money in this system. As KRS-One rhymed, "It's not about a salary, it's all about reality." It's about changing a system that doesn't work for the people who sweat and bleed on that field and who the fans are paying to see. No one buys a jersey with Jim Delany's name on the back.

At Texas A&M, I heard teammates complain about the system, but I didn't see them organizing themselves into any kind of resistance. Instead, I saw the opposite: players getting so twisted into knots of frustration that eventually they voted with their feet and just quit the team. People on campus would say, "Oh, dumb jocks. They can't handle school. They can't handle a campus environment." But I had teammates who wanted to go home, because they'd come from an all-Black area into this supremely white university, and they were in pain every day—physical and psychological pain. They tried to find their place in a cultural new world, and anyone who thinks that's easy has never had to do it. The team is no refuge, because the coach wants you to act a certain way and the school wants you to be a certain way, and for too many, it is hard not to succumb to it. For me, too, it was a very challenging situation because I went from diverse, mixed, beautiful Houston to College Station, where everything felt all-white. I always told the coaches that there should be more guidance to help players adjust to this environment.

What kept me sane was a small city just north of College Station called Bryan, Texas, which was very segregated, with an all-Black side of town. That's where I did most of my volunteer work, mentoring young people. I didn't even know the city existed until I took part in a community service project there for a class. You could feel the divide between Bryan and College Station, and Bryan helped me stay afloat. So did being at school with Martellus. We each had our own lives on campus, but we were together most of the time. We worked out together, studied together, lived together. That makes for a special bond because we've seen each other grow, all the way from babies through adolescence and into adulthood: truly from boys to men. Looking back, I feel so fortunate that we went to the same school. I had Martellus and Martellus had me. That's how we got through, but his presence was more like a cushion to catch me when I fell than a force field to protect me from the reality of racism in College Station.

On campus, sometimes people treated me like a hero, a god, because football is king in Texas. But other times, with the pads off, I was anything but. Once, I was near my dorm late at night, and a big drunk group of students started shouting, "Hey, n----r! Go back to Africa, n----r!" I wasn't mad so much as disappointed. I remember thinking, *Really? This is 2003. We're all in the middle of Texas, and we all know this place sucks. Why make it worse?*

I was half god, half property. But whichever half they were dealing with, I was never fully human. Is my being nerdy of interest? Do they celebrate things that have happened in the life of my community? You come to find out, painfully, that the answer is less "No" than "Why should we care?" College is supposed to be about intellectual and social growth, but when you play football, they don't want you to grow. At the time, I was studying religion on my own. I've always been and will always be a Christian. But I was exploring Islam. I was reading the Quran, as it mattered to me to figure out what religion I thought was right for me. I knew that a massive percentage of

African people who came to this country in chains were Muslim, before conversion. I knew I was a Christian because my ancestors were beaten to believe in Christ. I wanted to explore and discuss this: Did I really have these convictions with which I was raised, or were they just the legacy of slavery? These kinds of discussions made my coaches uncomfortable. Especially after the World Trade Center attacks on 9/11, people on campus weren't too thrilled with me, trying to engage people in the ideas I was reading in the Quran. I never became a Muslim. I just wanted to have those discussions. But that was too much.

Independent of football, life wasn't easy. Pele became pregnant with our first daughter, Peyton. Telling my dad was one of the hardest moments of my life. My father had left his football scholarship, remember, when my birth mother was pregnant, and now it looked like I was following that path. My football career could have ended then and there. I asked my dad, "What should I do? Should I leave school, get a job, and start working to support my daughter?" I didn't want to do that, and Pele didn't want me to do that either, yet my dad's word meant so much to me. He could have pushed me either way. But he insisted that I stay in school and try, somehow, to make parenting work with Pele. I was twenty and Pele was nineteen when Peyton was born. It was tough, commuting two hours back to Houston to see my love and my daughter, while we figured out how to be parents, and still maintaining the ten-hour day of the student-athlete.

It all came to a head when Peyton turned two on a game day. I wanted to leave after the fourth quarter and motor right to Houston for her little birthday party. The coaches told me that this was against the rules, that it was not professional. I clashed with the coaches because they didn't see me as a man; they didn't see what I was trying to do, in terms of being a good father to my child.

No one was going to come between my daughter and me. No way. I was suspended for a game, and it was the worst-feeling punishment in the world. If you get punished for partying or fighting or being a fool, I get it. But getting punished for trying to be a father to your child? It was a perfect example of how the coaches didn't try to understand what it was like to be a young Black man who was also a father, wanting to be there for his child.

I hear players say that their school did so much for them. I'm sure they feel that way, but I suspect there is a strong element of brainwashing as well, because in reality, they did so much more for the school. The players kept the darn lights on. But brainwashing athletes to play in the NCAA is an essential part of the NFL pipeline. We train to be professionals—on the field at least—and become recognizable brands before we even get to the league. That work is done without the NFL having to pay a dime. To make us into brands, they have to try to break us from being individuals or rebels. It's a sensory deprivation project. They move us, mostly, to small country towns or isolated campuses. They treat us like it's their job to "civilize" us, to change who we are. They want these schools to be like *Get Out*, if it were a sports movie, and we're handed a football before we enter the Sunken Place.

It gives the whole game away that college football is so popular in the SEC, where the legacy of Jim Crow and segregation is so powerful, and now they worship Black football players who make no money and are out there providing entertainment. The university people and the networks intentionally create this fake feel—they use the football field to miseducate people with a fictional portrayal of life off the field. The fiction is that because all these white student fans are cheering majority-Black teams, there is no more racism. It creates an illusion for both the fan and the player—the student and the student-athlete—so they don't have to face how messed up this country is. You're not Black on the field. You're a representative of your school. There's no New Jim Crow when you're on the field. There's no Donald Trump. There's no Trayvon Martin.

Ignored is how powerless we are when the pads come off, or that we are risking brain injury at an educational institution to entertain. I think people need to start realizing that the real world doesn't just reflect the field. It is the field. You watch *Remember the Titans* and it's this heartwarming Disney movie with Denzel Washington; I'm thinking, "Yeah, this is cool. They all got together." But at the end of the day, half the team had to eat outside. Everybody came to the game, the players bonded in the locker room, but it was still divided. Part of the mythology of sports is that people think it breaks down barriers and makes us more equal. That's miseducation. The only thing that's going to make us equal isn't sports. It's going to be people realizing that we're all human: everybody goes to the bathroom. Some of us sit, some of us stand up, but other than that, we do it exactly the same way.

My last year at Texas A&M, Martellus had already left for the pros, a year early, as one of the top tight ends in the country. My little bro Tellus was now a step ahead of me, out there in the NFL. I was proud of him, but that sucked for me. It was not easy without his big behind in my face. I had spent so much time with this one person my whole life—it was scary to now be alone, with Pele and Peyton a good distance away. I felt a little exposed; nobody to depend on, nobody I could talk to on a daily basis. Nobody I could share stories with.

The one positive was that having Martellus in the NFL meant I could hear from him about what it was like in the Big Show. Martellus had a rough rookie year. He was on the Dallas Cowboys, which sounds like a dream, but he was playing behind an all-pro tight end and future Hall of Famer, Jason Witten, and getting no love and no help from either their head coach, Jason Garrett, or Witten. As Martellus said, "I hated Jason Witten. I appreciated his game, but I always hated him."

It helped me realize that nobody is ever really ready for the NFL, no matter how physically gifted. As a kid, you see the glitz and the glamour, but you don't see the pressure to fulfill a job. You don't see all the stuff between game days, the grind. Martellus told me the straight truth. He said, "Man, this is a lot harder than anybody thinks. It's not just the money. You think you got the money and now you can lay with it, put it on your bed and roll around. It's more like, now you got the money, but now you gotta work twice as hard." I will always believe that Tellus's preview gave me an advantage over other NFL rookies, even if they were picked way ahead of me.

Without Martellus in College Station, I started reading more, thinking more, and speaking out more. My coaches looked at me like I was the devil. They didn't understand why I was walking around with a kufi on my head or why I was reading the Quran. They didn't understand why my locker was filled with books that had nothing to do with farming or the other easy classes on my schedule, why it was filled with *The Autobiography of Malcolm X* and *Letter from Birmingham Jail* by Dr. King. It scared them.

After my last year came the NFL draft. There I was, a future Pro Bowler, someone who in 2017 would be ranked as the seventeenth-best player in the league by *Sports Illustrated*, sitting with my family, watching the draft live on ESPN, a spread of food and drinks laid out. As the rounds went by and my name wasn't called, panic spread through me. I was getting calls all day from teams, saying, "We have our eyes on you. We're going to get you in the next round," but it wasn't happening. I got so agitated that right in the middle of the draft, my dad took me out fishing to relax, and I threw all the fishing rods in the water. When we got home, I curled up in my mother Miss Pennie's arms and cried. She patted my back, and when I looked at her and thought about everything she had taught me in life, it all made perfect sense. I didn't get drafted—I am sure of it— because NFL scouts talk to coaches to get the inside word on how "coachable" a player is, and I think they said I was "different." They probably said I asked too many questions. In any other job, an employer might think, "Hey! That's a deep thinker. That's a serious person. That's a plus." But not the NFL. They think that if you're in college and you aren't thinking and talking only about football, you aren't focused on "the job at hand." That's what they call it: "the job at hand." Yet it's a "job" in college: a job that doesn't pay us anything but disrespect, lifelong injuries, and the chance to fulfill a dream or fall into a pit.

Not getting drafted was a defining moment of my life. I'm usually upbeat about everything, happy to be alive, but I felt a deep dread and was worried about my future. I was watching with my mom, my dad, Pele—my fiancée at the time, preparing for us to build a life together—and we had our baby daughter. It was a very depressing twenty-four hours. Just one year before, we'd had the full, joyous experience with my brother on draft night: the suspense, the drama, the family, the food, and the thrill when he was picked in the second round. This was supposed to be another celebration. Instead, I just felt, *Wow, this is really happening. I'm not getting drafted.*

Within ten minutes, though, I went from depressed to fiercely ready because the phone started ringing. I got calls from a dozen different teams to come to their training camps. Just like that, I went from being undrafted to having my pick of cities. My dad looked at me like Yoda, and, as if seeing the future, said, "You gotta choose Seattle. I think Seattle is a good place for you. I think you'd be good there. That's the fit." He's not a fortune teller. He had sound reasons. My dad knows football, and he told me that Seattle played the same defensive schemes as Texas A&M, so I would have a head start on every defensive rookie in camp. And then, unlike most rookies, my head wouldn't be up my behind.

I trusted him, and Seattle was the dream spot for me. But I'll tell you this. It would not have mattered where I went, because not being drafted made me ready to bust through any door, any window, any skylight to make it. It pushed me to prove my doubters wrong, and it still pushes me at thirty-three, every workout, every practice, every game, because it's always on my mind.

SPORTS ARE NOT INTEGRATED

> I heard Jim Brown once say the gladiator can't
> change Rome. I love Jim Brown. But I disagree. I'll
> die trying, my brother.
>
> —**Arian Foster**

I have a sack dance I love to do. I gyrate my hips around like the great pro wrestling legend and lover Ravishing Rick Rude. I call it "Two angels dancing while chocolate is coming from the heavens on a nice Sunday morning." Now my wife won't let me do the dance anymore. Not because it was attracting too many admirers, but because it was costing us too much money: tens of thousands of dollars in fines.

They call the NFL the "No Fun League"—my brother has called it "N---as For Lease"—and that's the most brutally honest thing I've ever heard. There are aspects of playing that I love. I love my teammates—the brotherhood that the locker room brings together. I love coming out of the tunnel when we get introduced at home. I love winning the Super Bowl. I love the fans in Seattle. I love hitting quarterbacks. I love making enough money so I can help my family and my community. But the league itself, the violence you put your body through to play, is not fun. And as soon as you're done, you're gone. There's a quote from a boxer, Buster Mathis Jr., who asked his father if he should box or play football. His dad said, "Son, play football because nobody 'plays boxing.'" This needs to be amended. Nobody "plays" football, not anymore.

I should have gotten a clue at the NFL combine. At the time, just out of Texas A&M, I didn't really understand, and not even Martellus could prepare me. I felt the importance of it all: knowing this was a once-in-a-lifetime opportunity to make money and provide for my family. I thought it would be like a job interview with a Fortune 500 company, but then I walked into a room filled with a lot of older men. They gawked at me in a way I'd never been stared at in my life. I finally knew what it felt like to be objectified, the way so many women are. It was also clearly on me to impress them, to act like I was cool with the poking and prodding. I felt like they were Kardashians and I was an NBA starting center.

The best word for it is "awkward." I wish it had been awkward for everyone, not just the players. They should make the scouts sit there in their tighty whities and boxer shorts so we're all on the same level. Someone actually picked up my leg and measured my thigh. I was like, "Excuse me? Keep your eyes up here, sir." I thought, *Whoa, am I a piece of meat? Are they going to chop me up like cattle and sell me by the pound?* It reminded me of descriptions I'd read of slave auctions. People don't like to associate slavery with sports because of the money we're paid. But when you are made to feel as if you are property, and having grown men lift your arms to check your armpits, I don't really know what other comparison comes close.

The combine, though, was just mentally uncomfortable. You get through it and you move on. The real devil in this league is the pain: for the last seven years, I've been playing with a bad toe. I can't even wear some shoes, my foot hurts so bad. I know a toe isn't as serious as a concussion or a torn muscle, but I have to numb up part of my foot before every game. They stick a six-inch needle into my toe. They don't show that on *NFL Films Presents*. I'm glad they don't. It's gross. (Not my toe. My toe is beautiful.)

There are the hip surgeries, the knee surgeries, and the daily fear that you could just lose your brain; there is literally a bomb that could go off inside your skull on every play. That worry now hangs like a gray cloud over the game on Sundays. The word "concussion" softens what the injury really is. What we are talking about is a traumatic brain injury. When a normal person has a concussion, they're done for at least a week, resting at home in a room, usually in the dark, letting it get better. But for us, it's a bruise on your brain that never gets time to heal. In the NFL, we play on Sunday. No matter the rules and regulations, no matter how many posters they put on the locker room walls, we are pushed to do it by the toughest coach there is: that voice in our heads that tells us we don't have guaranteed contracts and this can all go away if we can't make it onto that field. Junior Seau played in the NFL for twenty years and was never diagnosed with a concussion, but it was found after he killed himself that he had CTE, and his family believed he'd had hundreds of concussions over the course of his career. I feel the same way. Of course I've had concussions. Just don't ask me how many, because if you ask me no questions, I'll tell you no lies.

Fans don't see this. Fantasy football isn't just a game they play on a computer. It's what they're watching on the field: the fantasy that we are disposable names and statistics. For years I've been trying to figure out what makes fantasy football so popular, and I've come to the conclusion that a lot of fans play fantasy because it allows them to look at us as if they are executives in an owner's box, and when they do that, it's easier not to see us as human. They see a player as a collection of statistics—and the numbers, not the human beings, tell the story. They don't see that a player has a wife or kids, or that real families are affected in the process. They don't see the pain. All they see is Sunday. I remember watching Sidney Rice, a great wide receiver, catch a touchdown and get knocked out of a game against the Chicago Bears. He was flattened in a way that made you wonder if he would ever be the same again. But everybody in the stadium roared, "Oh my god! We won!" And my man is still flat on the ground. He was concussed and he could easily have been dead.

I think people feel that because we are getting paid a lot, the risks we take are justifiable. This also means there is little empathy to be had. In other high-risk jobs, if someone gets killed or hurt, people mourn. But when a player has CTE, it's "He brought that on himself." I think about Junior Seau a lot because he was one of the greatest defensive players ever, and the respect he commanded throughout the league was phenomenal. He was held up as the ideal of what a player should be, yet he ended up stuck with a body that wouldn't physically work anymore and a brain that he couldn't recognize as his own. He stopped being himself, and he chose death.

Or Steve Gleason, the former New Orleans Saint, suffering with ALS, a brain disease that makes the muscles waste away, his body slowly breaking down. People love his story, but nobody wants to get deeply into it. No one wants to say that his current state may be connected to the sport. Or the study published in 2017 that examined 111 former NFL players' brains suspected of having CTE, and 110 had it. I don't want these people's names to be lost. The league doesn't want you to see how the hot dogs are made, but I don't want us to be hot dogs or statistics. You ever see what goes into a hot dog? Rat poop. We're better than that.

I think about CTE and bodily injuries all the time. I can say without shame that I'm scared every time I go out on the field that something possibly could go wrong, and I might leave my kids for good. That's my great fear, leaving my daughters and not seeing them grow. As I get older, and as I see them becoming these amazing young people, my fear is turning into a stone in my chest. I play with that in mind. There are some things I am simply not going to do, and trust me, I'm not alone. I'm not about the old-school hit, running my helmet into somebody. I'm not about to jump on the pile. I'm not about to leap over the line and land on my head. No way. I've got another life to live.

It's not just the fear of dying on the field but that when I'm forty-five or fifty years old, right when my daughters will be discovering new planets or inventing something fantastic or having children of their own, I won't be mentally able to enjoy their awesomeness.

I think about Cortez Kennedy, one of the best defensive players ever to play this game, one of the best Seahawks, and one of my friends. He died on May 23, 2017, and he was just forty-eight years old. I ate dinner with Cortez every Saturday night before home games for the last four or five years. He always had advice for me, on and off the field, and it staggered me when I heard he was gone. Cortez had an appointment to get his heart checked. Then he had a fatal heart attack the next day. He was a big man, and the strain on the heart for a former NFL player can be a more deadly by-product of this game than brain injuries. We loved Tez—not just the team, everybody. They played a video tribute for him before the first home game of 2017, and you could see fans crying in the stands. I still hear his voice before games, saying to me, "Go get it, young fella." As long as I hear those words, I feel like he's still with us.

For me, the fear is not just of death. It's fear of pain. And it's the fear that all the love I get from fans is more like the love they might give a steak. I'm loved until I'm eaten and all that's left is a bone. The hardest part as a player is knowing that people love you conditionally. Out of sight, out of mind. I like having retired players eat at my house. I feed them. I take care of them. I thank them and make a point of saying, "I appreciate everything you've done." It's because I understand what they did for us. They put their lives on the line. We wouldn't have a lot of the protections we have now if they hadn't taken risks. When older players stand up for better pensions, we need to follow them and support them because they are our parents, in a way. To do otherwise would be like saying, "Why should we celebrate Black History Month? I don't know any of those people. I don't know Martin Luther King. I don't know Harriet Tubman." You don't have to know them to know their impact. These players fought to get us everything from free agency to better medical care, and they haven't been taken care of properly.

I think about people like Hall of Fame running back Earl Campbell, Dwight Clark, Tony Dorsett, and Jim McMahon; I also think about the players who weren't considered superstars but still suffer. They say, "After you retire, everything hurts all the time." If you care about the person under the helmet, it will break your heart. When I see the older players limping, or their hands shaking before they're fifty, I feel scared, like I'm looking at my future. There are a lot of different figures out there of the percentage of players who die young or get severe CTE; let's say that it's 10 percent, which is crazy low, but for the sake of argument, we'll stick with it. If 10 percent of women were getting killed or if 10 percent of kids were getting kidnapped, it would be a national emergency. I get scared that I could be in that percentage. You have to keep that fear in you and acknowledge it, because that is what makes you human and able to realize, "I shouldn't be doing that."

The fear isn't just ours. Our families watch the games with their hearts in their throats every time we go down. One game, I went down just because I was dehydrated and my knee locked up. But watching up in the stands, my wife didn't know that. All she knew was I wasn't moving. Fans say, "Oh no! My fantasy team!" My wife and kids are saying, "Oh no. Our lives." I wish the NFL would do a better job of showing the public that we're not warriors but human beings. I hate that animated Fox NFL robot-soldier that gives the impression we are all like Robocop. It's not just the injuries. I want fans to know how it hurts to be apart from your family most of the year. They don't see the divide, the time a player spends away from his family. But then I wonder: If they did know, would fans care more about our well-being? Even those fans who don't ignore the toll on body and soul of playing this game think that we've made a deal with the devil, and maybe they're right. When you deal with the devil, sometimes it's great, but when the devil comes calling, don't expect any sympathy.

The NFL Reality Show

The pain of playing this game would be easier to swallow if we had the ability not only to play but, as former players, to have a voice: to become a general manager or even to own. But we don't. The NFL has no Black owners, and therefore this sport has yet to truly integrate. Fans might be paying to see the players, but the league is the owners. They make the decisions. They set the policies. They make the money with the extra zeroes. They're the ones holding up the Lombardi Trophy when it all ends. They are also around much longer. The NFL is more Jerry Jones than it's Michael Bennett or Richard Sherman. Then there are the general managers and head coaches, as of this writing overwhelmingly white. Of the thirty-two NFL teams, two have Black or Latino head coaches; five have Black general managers. It is still a sad, shamefully low number. If the NFL were really integrated, these figures would be different. The NFL needed what's called the Rooney Rule just to require owners to sit down with Black coaching candidates. They needed a rule just to talk to us. Not hire us. Talk to us.

This holds true across almost all of professional sports except in the NBA, where Michael Jordan is an owner. So you only have to be the greatest athlete ever and one of the most successful commercial brands in history, and you get to be an owner. We are integrated only on the level that people see on the field, yet all sports celebrate this half-view of integration. When Major League Baseball memorializes Jackie Robinson, they leave out that he wanted to be a manager or executive but they would not give him the opportunity.

In the NFL, we don't see Black former players in the *Monday Night Football* booth, but they're bringing back Hank Williams Jr.—a guy who performs with a big Confederate flag—to do the opening song. It shows not just their target audience but also their incredibly low opinion of those people. They assume that their white audience doesn't want to see Black faces or hear Black voices but loves a Confederate country singer. I think they're wrong, but owners are also conditioning people to be racially biased by sending these messages.

Even the word "owner" sounds terrible. I wish I could wave a wand or get one of those devices from *Men in Black* and change all our brains so we call them CEOs or chairmen of the board like in any other business, instead of owners. Players talk about how weird it is—a majority-Black sport, and we're talking about our "owners." If you think I'm being too sensitive, go to school tomorrow and call your principal your owner in conversation, and see how that feels. We owe our ancestors better than that. Players want to see a Black "owner" (there I go) simply because the hope is that they would be able to understand the reality of what it means to be a Black athlete. I wonder if the discussion around Colin Kaepernick—and if he would be signed—would be different if there were Black ownership.

Starting with more Black coaches would make a big difference. Not just in terms of opening closed doors, but for a better working environment for Black athletes. Many league executives, media members, coaches, and fans assume all Black players come from the same circumstances. They don't understand that although every Black person has experienced some kinds of racism, we come into this world from all kinds of backgrounds. I've had white coaches try to be a father figure to me, telling me how to tuck in my shirt or talk to the press or save my money. That's just patronizing. I've had to say, "Not only do I have a father, but I'm a father myself, so you can speak to me like a man." Even if I didn't have a father and had a tough upbringing, it would be hard for a white man to turn a Black man into a Black MAN because we go through so many different things.

It is true that a lot of African American players grew up in hard circumstances, in a certain type of America that most fans and definitely most coaches and execs don't understand. You take a kid from Miami-Dade County, an all-Black environment where poverty is life, and put them in a place like Texas A&M, where they're a tiny minority and everyone else has spare bills in their pocket. After four years, at twenty-two, a very small percentage of them will be pushed onto a pedestal and handed a sack of money, and most aren't remotely ready.

A lot of athletes, when they're speaking about their own powerlessness, particularly in NCAA or NFL football, call it a plantation. They talk about slavery. Inevitably, people slam them for that: "How dare you compare your life to slavery? How dare you call yourself a $40 million slave? You got money, so why are you saying that you feel like you have no voice?" But your money is tied to your silence. Your money is tied to walking the line. It's not like you created your own business, where if you wanted to say, "I don't like this. If you don't want to buy my product, don't buy my product," you could feel free to do that. Your product is you, so you have to look out for what people don't want you to say. You have no freedom to just be. You are not allowed to be successful unless you wear the mask.

You can see this so clearly in the curious case of Colin Kaepernick. By the time you read this, maybe Colin Kaepernick will be on a team, maybe not. Either way, it's shameful to the league that he was "whiteballed"—as 1968 Olympian John Carlos says, Colin was whiteballed, not blackballed—for standing up for his rights and the rights of his community. He's a great player who gives back, and his teammates love him. But the league and too many fans wanted to teach a lesson, not only to him but to every athlete who might want to step out of the box. Some awful quarterbacks with the arm strength of Donald Trump Jr. were signed while Kaepernick was left at home. Richard Sherman even read off the names in an interview. There has clearly been collusion to keep him off a team. Owners are scared of the relationships Colin is building and the issues he's raising. They are scared because his political views—that Black people shouldn't be killed in the streets by police and should be empowered—are threatening to white society. They don't want us to talk about this, even if it's happening in communities where we grew up and members of our families still live. I get it, as a business owner, but at some point this conversation has to be about humanity and our shared future, not just the bottom line.

When I first met Colin, I did not like him. Why? Because he was the quarterback on the 49ers. I never like any QB. But for a quarterback, he seemed cool. We always just said, "What's up." But when he took that knee, I called him, and we talked for the longest time about how to move forward, and how I could support him. In the off-season I got really close to him, talking to him more, because he was going through so much. I want him and everyone to know that I stand with him. He's my friend.

If I had to make a list of twenty players who might've taken a knee in the summer of 2016, he wouldn't have been on the list, because he was a QB. They have the most to lose. I'm glad it was Colin, because there is no position in sports more high-profile than quarterback, and he was able to handle the reaction. It wasn't just the death threats. He fielded the questions from the media, speaking truth every week for four months, knowing that this stand could end his career. And in the middle of it all he balled out. Players know he can play. Sixteen touchdowns and four picks on a terrible 49ers team. To be able to step into that spotlight and handle the pressure was amazing. To be able to ball out at the same time was legendary. To whiteball him after the fact only proves, as Colin has said, that he was right to speak out.

The stupidest comments about Colin—the part that sets my teeth on edge—were people in the media saying he can't be an athlete and an activist at the same time. It's like saying you can't be a father and a husband at the same time; you can't be a brother and an uncle at the same time. It's also insulting because now many of us consider ourselves athletes and activists. That's the reality of today, and the media needs to catch up to that reality. As for Colin, his ability to use his platform, play extremely well, and still be able to help the people shows nothing but leadership and nothing but greatness. It's what anyone should demand of a leader. You don't want a guy who just wants to be paid. You want someone with the soul of an organizer, who believes in the connections we can build between people. Don't think players don't support him. I know the media has planted the idea that there is a racial divide in locker rooms around Kaepernick, but I have love for players like Steven Hauschka, Chris Long, and Aaron Rodgers, who have stood up for him. We also know that his 49ers teammates voted to give Colin the team's Courage award. That says it all to me. The NFL holds up as leaders players who have been accused of rape, violence against women, and even manslaughter.

They're right in front of us, playing quarterback and winning Super Bowl MVP awards. I'd much rather call a leader someone who helps his community.

From talking to Kaepernick, I can tell you there is no doubt he wants to play. He also has no regrets about his choices. He just wishes the NFL would support him so he can keep sharing the message and inspire people to be different. I was walking with him through the streets of New York City, and I've never seen anything like it. I've been around a lot of people that we call "famous," but I've never seen people just glow in front of an athlete. They were all over him in an entirely different way. It wasn't because he was some quarterback superhero but because they knew he risked something and was paying a price for trying to make a change. People gave him a pound and thanked him, and he'd say, "Thank you" right back. It comes so naturally to him, and it's a beautiful thing to see. It says something very wrong about the sports world that there is no room for Colin Kaepernick because of what he believes in his heart.

It's not just players who get this. Two years ago I started raising my fist after sacks, as a tribute to John Carlos and Tommie Smith, the 1968 Olympians who raised their own fists on the medal stand in protest. When the NFL put out their "100 Best Players" list, I was on it, and in the video package, they showed me raising that fist four different times. They could've picked any image. They picked that pose, four times. They know what's up.

SOAP OPERA FOR MEN

> You're not thinking, "Hey, man, this guy got hurt—
> he's really physically hurt and he's going to take
> time to recover and it's probably going to affect his
> mental state and his physical state, and now he has a
> long, rigorous rehab." You're thinking, "Oh, man, he's
> messing up my fantasy team."... I think that's why
> you see the frustration from a lot of players, saying
> they don't care about your fantasy team. They don't
> care about how it affects your fantasy team because
> these are real players, this is real life. This is real life.
>
> **—Richard Sherman**

All my critiques of the NFL are real. But I know that people love this league, and I think above all else it's because the NFL is a soap opera for men. Please allow me to explain.

When you hear a couple of regular dudes talk about the NFL, it might start with stats or whether their team will make it to the playoffs, but before you know it, those fans have turned into a couple of old biddies gossiping about which player said what and who likes (or doesn't like) who. I get it. I don't mind it. In my experience, the female NFL fans are much more serious about Xs and Os and what goes into the game than the men are.

It's a little surreal when dudes get gossipy about our league, though, because those "NFL moments" people love are not just fun and games to us. On the Seahawks, they are what helped forge our brotherhood and created the most extraordinary locker room in sports. People still want to make small talk with us in Seattle about the Super Bowls, XLVIII and XLIX, and I am more than happy to do so. They were unforgettable experiences, but maybe not for the reasons people think.

In Super Bowl XLVIII, in 2014, we went all in against big bad Peyton Manning and the Denver Broncos. Peyton had thrown for something like fifty-five touchdowns that year, and the media was in love with him. Every commercial was Peyton's big head telling us what pizza to eat, what beer to drink, and what insurance to buy in case we got a heart attack from that nasty pizza. The Broncos were even favored by two and a half points, which is another way of saying that Las Vegas showed the world its behind for eternity, because we, of course, whooped them 43–8. It was one of the biggest butt-kickings in Super Bowl history and feels even better now, every time I see Peyton Manning playing golf with Donald Trump.

I feel like the team assembled that year was the NFL version of the 2017 Golden State Warriors: homegrown talent on cheap contracts with skills no one could match. It was unfair. The team was freak athlete after freak athlete after freak athlete. We had Kam Chancellor, Marshawn Lynch, Earl Thomas, Russell Wilson, Cliff Avril, Richard Sherman, Chris Clemons, and eventual Super Bowl MVP Malcolm Smith. But the freakiest freak—the one with a skill level so ridiculous we'd watch him in practice—was our wide receiver Percy Harvin. His physical abilities didn't make any sense. They did not compute. It was like watching an android come to our practices.

But it wasn't just the stars. We came at you in waves. Our backup cornerbacks eventually became $60 million or $70 million corners on other teams. Our backup linebacker was named the game's MVP and eventually signed to a $30 million free-agent deal. Our defensive line was stacked with monsters. Cliff Avril and I—both future Pro Bowlers—didn't even start. We had so many great players it felt unfair.

A lot of us thought it was hilarious that Vegas and many of the experts were favoring Denver going into the game. We knew we would win, and honestly, it wasn't just self-confidence. We knew we would win because their quarterback was Peyton Manning. We looked at tape and were like, "Yo! He can't throw deep anymore! That arm is like a rubber chicken!" With our corners, we knew: if Peyton couldn't throw deep, it was not going to work because we could cheat up on his receivers, and our defensive front seven were too fast to get taken on Peyton's dinky screens and short crossing patterns. He set a Super Bowl record for completions that day, and the Broncos still almost got shut out. That says it all. We tackled them every single time.

Without a garbage touchdown at the end, it would have been a shutout—the first of any Super Bowl.

That game changed NFL history because the Broncos' president, John Elway, looked at our team and decided to build his just like ours: a defensive-dominant team anchored by big cornerbacks and pass rushers everywhere. They won a Super Bowl two years later, with Peyton and Brock Osweiler under center. Elway even tried to sign me as a free agent after our Super Bowl win, but I was happy right where I was.

The next year, we were going for back-to-back Super Bowl titles and dynastic, legend status. Our eyes were so focused on the Super Bowl that we almost didn't make it to the big game, because of the NFC Championship Game against the Green Bay Packers and Aaron Rodgers. We were down 19–7 with four minutes left in the fourth quarter. I'd never heard our stadium, and our fans, "the 12s," that quiet. Seattle fans are as loud as it gets, and I could have had a conversation with somebody in the upper deck.

As stressful as it was, I knew we could win. Our quarterback, Russell Wilson, was such a big part of that feeling. Russ was having a terrible game. Just terrible. He may have been concussed early on by Packers linebacker Clay Matthews. But while I cared about his health, I wasn't concerned about his stats. I believe that if you give Russell Wilson enough time, he can win any game. He's proven it enough that I never have doubts. After playing the worst game of his life, Russ snapped back in the fourth quarter and overtime. It took a successful onside kick by my man

Hauschka and some more heroics, but we got through it in overtime, 28–22.

After the game, celebrating on the field, I was deliriously happy, knowing we were going back to the Super Bowl. I jumped on a policeman's bike and just started riding around the stadium. It was beautiful. I said later, "This is the only time a Black man can take a bike from a policeman and not get killed." It was one of those moments where I acted on my instinct to enjoy life to its fullest and just basked in the moment. I felt eleven years old. It was heaven.

The challenge of that game was in waiting for Russ to snap back, rather than being worried about Aaron Rodgers. For all his greatness, and Aaron Rodgers is a beast, we knew we could win if our offense started to click.

This would be as good a time as any to say that the best quarterback I've ever faced is Tom Brady. I know a lot of people say that, but I hope you know coming from me that it's no lie and it sucks to admit. I don't want to concede that any quarterback is good, other than my own. But if you play on the defensive front seven, you know: Peyton Manning is not even in the same discussion as Tom Brady. They call Peyton "cerebral," but Brady is right there with him, without all the performance art on the line. He's also as tough as a quarterback can be, maybe too tough. That's why his wife, Gisele, is worried about the number of concussions he's had. She gets it. He talks about his special "TB12" training regimen, and she goes public, like, "I don't care about this TB12 method. We've got three kids. You better make sure your brain works!"

Tom Brady was waiting for us in Super Bowl XLIX. People ask me about that game all the time, one of the best and most controversial in sports history. It's hard to talk about, but not because we lost in the final moments. That entire day is a little foggy for me. Just around that time, my wife's grandmother had passed away, and my best friend Rio's dad, Mark Alexander, had also recently passed. Mark was one of my best friends, too. I wore a cowboy hat on media day, and people thought I was messing around. But it was Mark's hat, and I wore it to honor him. Every time they showed that hat on television it made his family smile, and that's the only reason I wore it. There was so much pain on that day among the people I love most that the game seemed small, in the scheme of things. I never really dwelled on the fact that we lost. All that Super Bowl reminds me of is death and the fog I was in. Somehow I played well—knocking Brady down four times—but it's a faded memory in my mind, like a movie I barely remember.

What people always bring up is the last play for our offense. It was 28–24, New England, and we were one yard away from a touchdown with twenty-six seconds to play. One yard to a Super Bowl victory, and we threw an interception: the only interception thrown from the one-yard line that entire season. Watching that throw by Russell was gut-wrenching. Do I believe we should have run the ball? I think everybody believes that when you have a back like Marshawn Lynch, you run the ball. I was shocked, just like everyone watching at home. I thought we'd just hand it to Marshawn and pop the corks and call it a night. We were that close. It's not like we blew a 28–3 lead or anything.

But when we look back and wring our hands over that play call, way too often we forget to mention that this dude on the Patriots—Malcolm Butler—made an amazing interception to win them that Super Bowl. More than any game plan, football comes down to the instincts of great players. Everybody blames the throw, but Butler jumped that route out of nowhere, so you tip your cap. If he doesn't make that play, we win.

What bothers me are articles that say "the wound never healed" in the Seahawks locker room and, as they tell it, one game, four years ago, led to divisions on the team, as if one loss could be as severe as the wound on my stomach that wouldn't heal when I was a kid. It's ridiculous. Nobody on our team was still mad about the Super Bowl four years later. We were so past that it's ridiculous. But it's the media's job to plant a seed and create a narrative so the male fans can have their soap opera, especially in the off-season. The idea of a divided Seahawks team felt like a plot they were trying out to see if it was a soap opera that could grab an audience. Every year they need a soap, and the off-season is pilot season. In 2016 the narrative was "How can we distort what Kaepernick is doing into something that divides fans as much as possible?" Maybe this soap opera was about us because our team had players that would stand up and call out the lies. But at the end of the day, none of that really matters. All we need to do is play the game and try to play it right. If we win games along the way toward trying to reach our potential, then so be it.

When it comes to that Super Bowl, what people ask me about the most is the end of that game. Not the interception, but the real end of the game, when I got thrown out of the Super Bowl and lost my game check for beating Rob Gronkowski's behind. People ask if I threw him around because there was some kind of grudge, if he had been cheap-shotting me or going for my knees. It was nothing that dramatic. It had been a really tough week in my life, and I just hated losing to them. My brain told me, *You're about to lose this game, but you're not about to lose this fight.* Not a proud moment, but if you haven't been there, you don't know what it's like. Also, hell with Gronkowski.

After the game, I mourned. Not the game loss, but the loss of the people who'd left this world. Like my Popo said: "Death is death."

In February 2017, I was back on the Super Bowl field. Not with the Seahawks, obviously, but with Martellus, who had just won with the Patriots over the Falcons. He played like a monster among men, and they came back from a 28–3 deficit. That makes the way we lost our Super Bowl look like a very small plate of potatoes. The Falcons yakked that up, but the Patriots also had to capitalize on every single opportunity, with no margin for error, and score on every drive in the second half. Martellus was in the middle of that action. I was super happy for him. I felt the same way I had when we won, and I cried. I didn't even care that it was with the Patriots. I was so proud of him because he put in the work. We both did the impossible—now two brothers from a Louisiana farm, with big mouths they always said would hold us back, have got rings. We did what Dan Marino couldn't do. We did what Michael Vick couldn't do. We did what Jim Kelly,

Barry Sanders, and Bruce Smith couldn't do. Those guys are considered the best, but they never climbed the mountain that the Bennett brothers climbed. They might have the best individual stats, but they've never been on a team that experienced greatness with everybody reaching a common goal. All of us put in the work together. When they hand out that trophy, they aren't just talking about one of us. Every single person on our team gave a piece of themselves to make it happen. And I love that Martellus got to experience that.

I'm being honest when I say I didn't even care that it was with the Patriots. The Patriots have earned every respect. Bill Belichick is so far ahead of his time in how he understands the game. Belichick is also more like Pete Carroll than people know. They are so opposite in superficial style, it's as if they have come all the way around the circle to meet. Pete Carroll is like the high school teacher who listens and wants you to be yourself and share what you are thinking, the one who rolls up his sleeves and turns his chair around to sit. His message is that you can be yourself as long as you show up on time and do the work. Belichick is like the high school teacher who literally does not give a care what you do in his classroom. He's in his own world. Like a mean Professor Dumbledore, he sees all and knows all, but he's not smiling. You can do whatever you want as long as you show up on time and do the work. Same ends, different means.

Belichick and Carroll know how to reach players, and they also understand the game. A lot of coaches don't meet that description, and usually it's because their daddy or granddaddy had power in the NFL. It's worse than an Ivy League college. You've got great guys like Sherman Smith, our former running backs coach, who was on the NFL sidelines for more than twenty years and, before that, played in the league for eight years—but never had an opportunity even to be an offensive coordinator. So many qualified people have never had a chance to lead a team because they don't have legacy status. It's an elitist aspect of the sport that no one wants to talk about. And these legacy coaches, far more often than not, tend to suck, because they have no one's respect. Because they never really had to get their hands in the dirt, they, in particular, don't understand that when you're a veteran you basically coach yourself. I watch tape on my own or with the line to learn what needs to be done. We figure it out.

When I watch the best defensive linemen, I don't look at how the play ends or just how quickly they come off the ball. I'm looking at their hands. What is the angle of his hands on the turf? How are his feet moving when his hands hit the offensive line? Are his hands moving in rhythm with his feet? How quickly does he run to the ball? How does he work his forearms to get the lineman off balance? It's all martial arts to me: leverage, balance, and using their momentum against them. When I play, I always look at the eyes of the person blocking me: Where are his eyes? What are they telling me? Also, if I focus on eyes, I don't think about the fact that I'm about to run into a brick wall with legs for the next ninety minutes.

I also like looking at old tape of the people who, when it comes to technique, we might as well call the Magnificent Seven: Warren Sapp, Alan Page, John Abraham, Justin Tuck, Dwight Freeney, Richard Seymour, and Shaun Ellis. I love watching tape of those guys playing. I don't even care about the score of a game or where the ball is on the field. I just love studying them and their instincts. Most fans and a lot of sportswriters just look at the stats. But players know that stats don't tell the true story. I study players like Brandon Graham, a defensive end for the Philadelphia Eagles. Fans outside of Philly barely know who Brandon Graham is because he never had big sacks totals, but I think he's one of the better defensive ends in the league.

We talk about game planning, training, and study; no doubt all of that matters. But instincts are a massive part of this game: case in point, Malcolm Butler making that interception in the Super Bowl. The greatest players are the most instinctual players. There have been outstanding physical specimens who break all the combine records, but they don't have instincts and are first-round busts. They might have the skill, but they don't know when to strike. They've got no cobra in them. They might make all the textbook movements, but because they didn't set up the kill in the right way, they can't finish. They can't deliver that moment when you knock your blocker off balance and make the play. I live for the setup: that coiled moment before it's time to go cobra. Sometimes you get into a game and you can just feel where the ball is going and whether it's going to be a run or a pass. You then slide off the lineman and no matter how good he is, he becomes just a big dude with his hands on his hips, explaining to his quarterback how he just got played.

Instincts for a lineman matter so much more than whatever scheme we might have cooked up. Cliff Avril and I would sometimes improvise our plan of attack and speak to each other on the spot, from play to play, about what we want to do. Those of us up front develop a feeling for the offensive line over the course of a game that coaches don't get. That's when the instincts take over. I'm always focused on the six inches in front of my face and beating that one offensive lineman right in front of me. If you aren't in my face, I'm not thinking about you. It's why I can say I've never been scared of any quarterback or offensive lineman, and I've never been scared of any running back. Of course, I never had to play against Marshawn Lynch. Tackling him might change my mind. As far as offensive linemen go, Walter Jones, who played his whole career with the Seahawks, is the only person who's really ever blocked me. I thought, "That man is too strong to be human. I'm so happy he's on my team!" But no one I play against makes me nervous.

It blows my mind that "undrafted me" is on the short list of top NFL defensive linemen, according to NFL.com. To me, J. J. Watt, Cliff Avril, Von Miller, and Gerald McCoy are the best at what they do up front, and it's an honor even to be mentioned in their company. I try not to think about it, because I worry that if I bask in the praise I'll lay off the hard work, so I try to keep my mind on my roots. When I'm lifting weights and training, if I said to myself, "Life is beautiful. Hey, who's in the mood for pie?," I'd tap out in ten minutes. Instead, I crunch my jaw together and say, "I'm undrafted. They don't care about me. Heck with this system." That helps me get to the next level. It also pushes me to look at tape when I'd rather be watching *The Proud Family* with my youngest.

I know I've been doing this a long time because now, when I work out, the best part is finishing. The hardest part is to continuously dedicate myself. It's not age. It's because the more successes you have, the more you hear a voice suggesting sweetly and seductively to rest on those laurels and just skip it or dog it, go half-assed. That voice asks you, "Why are you working that hard? You got it!" But to be great, you have to continuously put yourself in the mind-set where you *don't* got it. You have to think about the times you were hungry, you were struggling, you were a kid being pushed around. You have to come up with the darkest thoughts possible—I think about almost dying from my ruptured appendix and blood poisoning—and then use that to motivate yourself, every day. Every weight room should have a psychiatrist, because people dredge up painful stuff just to keep going. That's how I motivate myself. I get traumatized and go to the gym with the attitude that the gym owes me something, like it's my enemy. I speak to my body like it's a separate person from the voices in my brain. I say, "Body, you're going to do exactly what I want you to do, every single time I get in the gym." That's the kind of mind-set you have to possess. You have to whip yourself to push past the nagging injuries and build your body to the point it can sustain not only the intensity of the workouts but also the intensity of the sport.

It's a cliché, but it's god's truth: every Sunday we are involved in the physical equivalent of a car crash. Sometimes more than one. I heard NFL owner Terry Pegula, of the Bills, mock the idea of players' getting brain injuries in our sport, saying, "You can be driving your car and get a concussion in an accident. I don't want to discuss the relevance of it in football." This is so ignorant. The NFL consists of voluntary car crashes, one after the other, for the entertainment of others. Players say that they're willing to "die on the field" and people cheer. It's self-destruction, but the "warrior code" is real. It might sound like lies, but the people who say it aren't lying. The "warrior code" can kill you. It's unique to football, which is part of the appeal. I watch the NBA and guys sit out indefinitely for a pulled hamstring, but I've seen guys play through stuff you could never imagine a human being playing through. Forget concussions. Everyone plays with concussions. But to see people play entire games with bone on bone in their knees or dislocated shoulders, thumbs, fingers, hips, torn ligaments, all kinds of things, is to see a mix of brave and crazy.

I've seen players go out there handicapped, and then they pay the price. Too many guys I see getting crippled in slow motion, and I feel like I can see their future. Watching guys go through those injuries, get pushed to levels their bodies cannot handle, you understand why so many players suffer when it's all done. I tell myself that when I'm working out, I'm not just prepping for next season but for retirement. I want to stay lean and have good eating habits now, so I can function later in life.

This is where the brotherhood can hurt you. You are going to have brothers you love to death who try to push you to play through an injury. They say, "We need you." And you want to be there for them. It's not some coach telling you this in a speech he stole from Al Pacino in *Any Given Sunday*. It's your teammates. Organizations can use the brotherhood mind-set against you as well. They'll coax you to take that cheaper contract or come back earlier from injury. They go for your most sensitive spot: the desire to be with the people you care about long term. But if you get hurt, your locker will be cleaned out by breakfast, or if you're lucky, lunch.

Then there are people in the brotherhood who urge you in the other direction. They say, "You need a life. You have a family, man, you've got kids. Don't come back unless you're ready. Do not step on that field unless you are ready to go. Don't do it. Don't trust any doctor but the one you hire." In the words of Hall of Fame linebacker Mike Singletary, "Can't do it. Won't do it!" That's what a real brother says. Don't go out there, unless and until you're ready. We need more brothers to look out for each other in this way.

You look around the locker room, and so many players moving toward the end of their careers are walking around with huge muscles, but on the inside they are torn apart. It's not just their bodies. Mentally they're not there anymore, because for their whole lives, sport has defined them: everything they have in life is because of this sport. People love you because of the way you jump and run; when you lose it, you no longer mean anything. That's the hardest part: to look at your body and feel in your bones that it can't do what it was once able to do, and know that your value and worth in the eyes of others will be diminished. The question is, how can we free ourselves from having our physical ability be the final word on how we see ourselves?

But we as players don't operate this way, and that's why so many experience intense suffering in retirement. People's minds are broken not just because of concussions but because they don't understand that an athlete needs to build up an independent sense of worth and purpose so there's something to move on to after that last game check. It's the toughest task, because while you're playing, fans and management and coaches don't want you to evolve. They want you to be the same person you were when you got signed as a rookie. Why do people feel like athletes need to be stuck in their place in life? The only thing you can do is run fast, jump high, and sell some products. You can't go out and do other stuff. This can make retired players in their thirties already feel empty and isolated—you wake up in the morning and don't even know how to start the day. It opens you up for depression, drug addiction, and worse.

Today I'm going to work on this book, take my kids to the beach, attend a meeting about building a school in Africa, and run a science program for kids. You have to be able to do projects that impact the world or you'll devolve into dust. You've got be a human being. Enjoy yourself. It's your life!

Martellus is my role model for this. He writes children's books, he runs a business and develops apps. Ever since we were kids, he's been creative. He used to collect the bikes we got for Christmas, get out tools, take the bikes apart, and sell the parts. It was amazing. He took them all to school and sold them. Like LeBron, he's a mogul who's socially conscious.

Martellus is my actual brother, but my team is my brotherhood. They have sustained me, gotten me through the minefield of the NFL, and taught me to redefine how I understand family. It took a combination of a special city, a special coach, and a remarkable group of young men to make that a reality.

BROTHERHOOD

Ask not what your teammates can do for you; ask
what you can do for your teammates.

—Magic Johnson

I went into the NFL thinking the goal was to get in, kick
butt, and get out. I didn't need to make friends. I just needed
to provide for my family and move on. I learned this would
also be the place where I'd find the truth about what I could
be, and where I'd meet the people without whom I cannot imagine my life. It's not the championships or the Pro
Bowls. It's the blood relationships that the intensity of this
league allows you to build with the people around you.

I signed with the Seattle Seahawks in April 2009. Walking into that locker room for the first time, I felt so much
doubt. When you are undrafted, the question *Do I belong here?*
shadows your every step. But then I saw people I knew from
college, people I'd competed against, and they were kind to
me. No one made me feel like I had snuck in the back door.
All of a sudden, I was just another rookie, and that's exactly

what I needed to believe. According to my coaches, I played like a first-round draft pick in preseason. Then, I was the last cut in training camp, and it rocked me. I was walking around in a fog. The team said they would re-sign me as soon as possible if I stuck around, but I couldn't afford to take that chance. I signed with the Tampa Bay Buccaneers and balled out. But Tampa was rough on Pele and me. We were a young couple, strangers in a strange land. Everyone assumed we were from somewhere in Latin America and spoke to us in Spanish. I love my Latinx sisters and brothers, but it sucks when people try to talk to you, trying to make friends or something, and you don't know how to respond. We were trying to build our family in a new city without a community.

I was also on a losing team, but I took my job so seriously, as prepared by Tellus, that my sole focus was on proving myself. I was trying to win respect as a player who wasn't drafted, and I needed to feed my family, so that pushed me harder than most. I learned how to be a pro in Tampa, thanks to two veterans who might seem as different as Jekyll and Hyde in this league: Ronde Barber and Albert Haynesworth. Ronde Barber was a cornerback and, in my opinion, should be on the fast track to the Hall of Fame. His reputation as one of the most professional, personable people in the league is absolutely deserved. Albert Haynesworth was a defensive lineman, with as many physical gifts as anyone in the league: six feet six and 350 pounds of strength and speed. Big Albert was the league's Defensive Player of the Year in 2008, but he is known to fans as someone who has gotten in trouble off the playing field and as the player who once stomped on an offensive lineman's head, which, while I've never done it . . . I can understand.

The public perceptions of Ronde and Albert don't matter to me. They were my mentors. I still call Ronde Barber, when I see him, "Big Bro." The way he talked to me, seeing the way he trained and the way he took care of himself, was like taking a master class in being a professional. Albert Haynesworth took me aside and taught me the tricks about how to play on the line, things coaches don't know unless they played. He also advised me to be smart with my money, something every player should learn, especially considering the statistics about how many NFL players end up broke. Albert took me and another young player, Gerald McCoy, the third overall pick in the 2010 draft, under his wing—two future Pro Bowlers—and made us into a couple of young beasts. Gerald McCoy is a really good person and friend. We thought we'd be in Tampa together forever, like Warren Sapp and Simeon Rice. We talk once a week, and to this day, we'll see each other and say, "Man, if they'd just kept us together, people would have talked about our Tampa legacy forever."

But when I became a free agent in 2013, I went right back to Seattle, signing a one-year deal even though I had better, longer-term offers from other teams. People ask me if that was a tough decision, given the way I was cut from Seahawks training camp as a rookie, but the truth is that even after four years in Tampa, I never stopped thinking about Seattle or its team. While on the Bucs I even had a dream that I would make it back to the Emerald City and we would win a Super

Bowl. I wanted to see that dream through. Seattle's vibe had connected with me: new ways of thinking, new ways of doing things. I saw people collaborating and respecting others for being different. That was so important to me and reflected the kind of life I wanted for my family.

The move back was good for Pele, also, given her family's roots in the Pacific Islands. If that's your background, Seattle is one of the few cities in this country, outside of Hawaii, where you have some representation and cultural connections. We wanted that not just for us but for our babies, too. Texas was so Black and white, and Florida was even worse. I was in Florida when Trayvon Martin was killed. I'll talk more about that later, but for now I'll say that it was hellish to live through. Seattle instead put out an energy, with different kinds of people mixing it up—Black, white, brown—in a way that felt more open and less conservative than anything I had experienced. I thought, "Man, I could really live here for the rest of my life." It was just perfect for me. I'm convinced the feel of the city is one of the reasons why our locker room was unique in the NFL.

When I played in Seattle, the locker room was like a brotherhood. It was a place where we could talk politics or talk smack, and the coaches believed strongly that we needed to be ourselves. We needed to be men. We didn't "belong to the team," like one jerky columnist once wrote about me. We belonged to ourselves and to each other. In some other NFL locker rooms, if that kind of political environment developed and people were talking about real life in emotional voices, coaches would step in to say, "Don't bring those politics in here." That's a fake way of trying to keep people in a box. It's also insulting: telling a group of grown men basically not to talk to each other. Many players are willing to accept those kinds of terms on their humanity. But if a coach said to me, "I don't want you saying those things," I'd be like, "Then stop listening. It's our locker room. Take your butt upstairs." In our locker room, we didn't play that.

Our team was different. We talked about race issues. We talked about the NCAA. We talked about how to support one another's foundation work. When people signed with our team and saw how community based the Seahawks were, and how we talked to one another, they would be overwhelmed: "Wow, your team pushes you to be out there, they push you to give back." We'd reply, "No! Our team doesn't push us to do it. We push ourselves."

Early on in Seattle, I joked, "My only friends on the team are Benjamin and Franklin." That was me trying to be funny. It also couldn't have been further from the truth. My teammates in Seattle were my brothers. Most people go to work and hate their coworkers or never get to know them. They spend more time with their coworkers than with their own kids, but they never learn what makes them tick. This is one of the very few jobs where you need to be intertwined with those other people spiritually, because every movement you make has an end result—if you win or if you lose, if you walk off the field or if you're carried off.

We went from teammates to brothers, even though our backgrounds, educations, and even home countries were different. I can't tell you how emotional it was for me when Justin Britt, our offensive lineman and a leader in our locker room, a white dude from Lebanon, Missouri, put his hand on my shoulder while I sat during the anthem during the preseason of 2017. It felt like the classic football movie *Brian's Song*, like we were Gale Sayers and Brian Piccolo, except neither of us had to die. Afterward, Justin said to the media, "I'm going to continue talking with Mike and exploring and just helping myself understand things. I wanted to take a first step tonight. And that's what I felt like I did." He even told the press that if he didn't see things getting better in this country, he'd sit with me. That's a brother.

I think about Cliff Avril, how we worked together in this intense environment and got to know each other's families. We started out with different ideas about how to bring change into the world, and we've chosen to intertwine them because we're both passionate about helping people. He's seen what I do in Seattle, and I've gone with him to Haiti to see the remarkable work he does there. We may approach things differently, but we share the same soul.

The journey of moving from teammates to brothers is like nothing else. Yes, ego and money can get in the way. It takes the right people, the right team, and the right city, but when everything comes together it's a blessing. Every time you go out there and take the field, you don't just represent your team or your city. You represent each other in a way that's personal. I knew that if I made a mistake, Cliff Avril could get hurt, and then I'd have to look his wife, Tia, and their children in the eyes. When you reach that level of brotherhood, I truly believe that's when you win. You lose the ego, and it stops being about you. It's about the people around you. People get it backward and think winning is the end goal. But when the goal is brotherhood, the winning will come and mean so much more. Your locker room isn't just a place with coworkers or people trying to make bank. You transcend the money and the praise that come with it. You are tied to one another spiritually and physically, not just at the workplace but outside the workplace as well. You feel their pain when they get injured. You cry with their wives. You mourn with them when members of their family pass. You work on their projects, you go to their children's birthday parties, their anniversary celebrations, and you leave this league as someone more than when you entered.

Let's talk about who made up the core of this brotherhood in Seattle. I should say that one of the reasons we were like brothers is because a lot of us had chips on our shoulders. "Chip" doesn't even do it justice. Call it a boulder. Call it Pikes Peak. We were a team of Pro Bowlers and Super Bowl champions, but very few of us were high draft picks. We were disrespected and dismissed, and we would play mad on Sunday, trying to remind every team that they done messed up by passing us by. Trust me, that would go from players whose chip was obvious because they played with a mean mug all the way to the quarterback who was the smiling face of our franchise.

That's Russell Wilson. If you had never watched the NFL and I told you our quarterback was a Pro Bowler, perennial MVP candidate, Super Bowl champion, and a college All-American who set the NCAA record for passing efficiency, you'd think he was some kind of golden child, number-one draft pick: Archie Manning's other son.

But Russell Wilson was a third-rounder—and he was actually picked behind a punter. A punter! The main reason for that, in my opinion, is that a lot of NFL scouts just don't know their business. They are risk averse, scared of doing something different or thinking outside a very tiny box. They have a type, and if you don't fit that type you might as well not play. Russell Wilson is five feet ten, and that was enough for no one to take him seriously. Scouts have lost jobs that they would have right now if they had just picked Russell Wilson.

Beyond the play, Russ was central to this brotherhood. I saw Russ evolving every year. I love him because he laid claim to his own style of leadership and his own way of looking at the world. He is so genuine that people who don't know him think he's fake, which is ironic. He's himself. It's crazy that people call him phony. One thing about an NFL locker room: you know who the phonies are within five minutes. If Russ were screaming like Tom Brady, with spit flying out of the corner of his mouth, that would be phony. Russ is himself. It's like Muhammad Ali said: "I don't have to be what you want me to be."

Somehow a rumor became a big media story—that defensive players were mad because Coach Carroll "protected" Russell Wilson and treated him differently. The whole thing was just stupid. Everybody in the world is treated differently, in some way or another. Nobody is treated exactly the same. Even when you've got kids, you don't treat every kid the same way. Also, Russ is a quarterback, and *all quarterbacks* are treated differently. Every team I've been on, from flag football on up, the quarterback has been treated differently. Not in a bad way. They've got a different sort of relationship with the offensive coordinator. I don't like to talk to the defensive coordinator. Just tell me the play and let me do my job. But the QB and offensive coordinator have to be closer than brothers: they have to share a brain in order to understand the vision and what the other is doing.

Russ is a good friend and good people, and kids are attracted to him like he's covered in candy. My oldest daughter told me Russell Wilson was her favorite player. That was too much. I took her TV. I said, "Russell Wilson can buy you a new TV."

But I do have to give Russ credit. He helped me get a table when I called a restaurant and they were all booked up. I called them back a few minutes later and said, "Hey, this is Russell Wilson. I'll be attending your restaurant today. Do you have any tables?"

And the hostess was like, "Yes! We can make a table for you! You were 22 for 30 the other night, 130 quarterback rating!" She knew every stat.

When I got to the restaurant with my wife and kids, I said, "Oh, thank you. I'm Russell Wilson."

She was like, "Good joke."

I said, "Gotcha." She took me to the table and it was separated with a velvet rope—a makeshift VIP section. They had sparkling water and everything.

My brother was also Steven Hauschka, our former kicker. I missed Hauschka after they cut him. The only NFL jersey I have in my house, other than my own, is Steven Hauschka's. People think that being the place kicker is the simplest job on the team, but to me, you have to have a very special mind. The game is on your feet several times a season, and you're only as good as your last kick. Adam Vinatieri won two Super Bowls on the last play, but if he'd missed his final field goal with the game on the line, he'd be a bum.

Hauschka is a really cool dude. I think of Hauschka and Justin Britt in very similar ways. One is a kicker and the other is six feet six and 320 pounds, but they are both my brothers. They have taught me that there are times when race doesn't play a part in our interpersonal relations, and we all just become spiritual. People are friends simply because they have the same moral code. They believe in the same things because they are good people. Not on a shallow level, but on the level of being vulnerable, really getting to know somebody, and being there for each other. My white brothers are important to everything that we do, especially in confronting racism and what divides us. I want them standing with me, as Hauschka did when he was on the team and as Britt did on the sideline.

Marshawn Lynch was my brother. He is the best running back I've ever seen, a star at Cal–Berkeley, a star in Buffalo, and then a legend with the Seahawks. He retired for a year but then came back and played on his hometown team, the Oakland Raiders. Marshawn sat for the anthem the night before I did, holding an unripe banana. The significance of the banana is known only to Marshawn. After that preseason game, people were joking that maybe he came out of retirement just so he could sit for the anthem, that he'd felt left out in 2016.

Marshawn is an example of somebody people judge based on how he looks and talks, and they don't understand the depth of who he really is or what he is saying. He rocks that look because it's true to who he is. Mentally and spiritually, he's as good a dude as I've ever known. He works for his community and his teammates, and whenever you call him, he answers the phone. He could be mayor of Oakland just by having his name on the ballot. I think he's a great leader, who people might misunderstand much of the time, but what's cool is that he doesn't even care. When he sat for the anthem in the 2017 preseason, a reporter said to him, "Let's talk about the elephant in the room." And Marshawn replied, "I think that elephant just left the room 'cause a little mouse ran in here. Didn't they say elephants are scared of mouses or something? That MFer left, cousin." What does that mean? I have no idea, and that's kind of what makes it perfect.

We also saw it before the Seahawks Super Bowl, when he said, "I'm just here so I don't get fined" to the media, over and over again. I loved that. He just stayed true to who he is. He's the only person I've ever known who didn't say anything to the media and somehow got more commercials out of it. By saying nothing, he inspired the rest of us to speak our minds. He defies all expectations, and there are NFL fans who will never get that. But great leaders don't conform to the norms, and he defies the norms every time.

Marshawn is obviously very charismatic on the field, and that's where it starts. His two "Beastquake" runs, where he ran through the entire Saints team and then the entire Cardinals team, were like nothing I've ever seen on an NFL field. His big "Beastquake 2" run was the best touchdown I've ever seen. Afterward, I said he ran that like he was running to the North for freedom. We hadn't seen a run like that since the Underground Railroad. When he was really motoring, I'd see linebackers and safeties make "business decisions" to whiff on tackles instead of letting Marshawn hit them. That on-field charisma carried over to our locker room. His vibe was so intense that when he left a room you'd feel the void. When I walked past where his locker used to be, it's like I felt his ghost. It was beautiful and creepy. But I'm not scared of ghosts, so it was cool.

Richard Sherman was our shutdown corner and a future Hall of Famer, and one of the most outspoken players in the game. He's a four-time Pro Bowler who made the journey from Compton to Stanford, one of the smartest people in any room he's in. He was also a fifth-round draft pick in 2011 and has proven himself the best corner in that draft, so he's got that chip on his shoulder, also. We share a lot because Richard believes he was drafted so late because his coaches talked him down to NFL scouts for being outspoken. Richard is more cerebral than any player I've lined up with. You will never beat his mind on the field. His mind is tough to beat off the field, too. Richard has pushed me to think more deeply about what I'm doing and what I'm thinking. He has spoken out about the NCAA and about racism, and he's written essays for *Sports Illustrated* challenging journalists to think through their use of words like "thug" and "posse" when they write about Black athletes. No doubt he has changed the language of sports journalism.

Richard also gives back to the community in ways that go unreported. If I'm doing a project and working with kids, I know I can get Richard—bam—on FaceTime and see their faces light up. I talk to Sherm all the time because he's just who he is and I love him. We also had a public debate about the Black Lives Matter movement that cemented our bond, but we'll get to that.

Kam Chancellor, our strong safety, was somehow also a fifth-round draft pick and is another future Hall of Famer from our defense. He was central to why they called our secondary the Legion of Boom, because when Kam hit you, you stayed hit: he had linebacker size and safety speed. When Kam was having contract issues, I did what you're not supposed to do and spoke directly on national television to the Seahawks' owner, the late Paul Allen, to say, "Pay this man!" I just wanted to show Kam I had his back and that he should get his money. A lot of people have said, "I can't believe you called out your owner on national television. Nobody's ever done anything like that." But I thought, *Hey, Paul Allen said that he respects me for being me, so I'll just keep being me and see how that goes.*

Doug Baldwin is one of the best wide receivers in the sport. He's another undrafted Pro Bowler on the Seahawks. We might have had the most Pro Bowlers drafted in the fifth round or later on one team in NFL history. He's also out of Stanford, like Richard. Doug has been outspoken from the jump, addressing issues like police reform and mass imprisonment and how they affect the Black community. He is driven by religious principles and the social gospel to make the world a better place. Doug practices his politics differently than I do, and that's cool. He wants change and he tries to make it happen by sitting down with politicians and police chiefs. A lot of us are wrestling with how to go from tweeting about change or giving an interview to actually seeing it happen and sustain itself. I'm trying to do it grassroots, to make change through community organizing. I don't think I'm right and he's wrong for taking his own path. It's like the three legs on a stool; we need all of them. We need people who are outspoken in interviews. We need folks sitting across from the powerful. And we need people at the grassroots.

I also had so much respect for Doug when he wrote this condemnation of the 2016 election and just put himself out there, vulnerable. Here is a portion of his essay:

> The fact is that we are not currently living in a democracy. The fact is that the 1% of the 1% buy politicians and write policies. They control the gathering/distribution of wealth and power by distracting us with the importance of keeping up with the Kardashians. We've become a society [so] concerned with being individuals and looking out for oneself that we have forgotten the meaning of democracy. I know my thoughts may be concerning to some, but being on both sides of the coin has given me a great perspective. It's scary to think that we are on a path to granting the wealthiest people in the world the power to control the masses. And maybe that is why so many people were willing to vote for a president that didn't meet previous expectations for a president. The way of life of many Americans is being destroyed. Inequality is greater than it has ever been. And solidarity is nowhere to be found. The dream that America once promised has become a nightmare for a lot of people. The lack of hope and empathy has created despair and pain. Empathy and sympathy for not only your fellow American but your fellow human has been lost. We are more concerned with status [by] any means.

I mean . . . wow.

Jeremy Lane was our cornerback, a sixth-round draft pick who became one of the top corners in the league. He took a knee during the anthem, he sat down, and he turned his back, facing Justin Britt and myself. Jeremy's outspokenness didn't surprise me at all. He's a Black man from East Texas. You grow up in Tyler, Texas, you know racism is real. You don't need anybody to teach you.

Earl Thomas, our other future Hall of Famer safety, was the outlier—he was actually drafted in the first round. Earl was so good at the University of Texas that not even an NFL GM could mess up his selection, although there were players picked ahead of him who are now out of the league. Earl is a quiet assassin. He's quiet until you get to know him, and then he starts opening up. I texted him when I traded in my car for a Tesla: "You're still getting gas, Earl. I'm electric, I'm trying to save the world!" What I love about him is that in both football and life, the man is a sponge, soaking up all the information in the room. It's been great to see him become a leader.

Frank Clark is a player we need to discuss. He's a linebacker we drafted in the second round, in 2015, and a very special talent. Frank came from a rough background. He grew up homeless. He has a history of violence against women, from back in college, an issue that means a great deal to me. But Frank's trying to change. He's trying to understand. He could very easily be a broken person by now. That he is not broken and continues to try to be better means, I believe, that he will stay on a trajectory to become a leader and reach kids who can't otherwise be reached. He needs to be at peace with his past, make amends, and move forward. By virtue of being on my team, he's also family, and when you are family, you help people to change and stand behind them on their journey. I don't know what pushing people away accomplishes, especially when they're young and need guidance. Frank sat with me when I sat for the anthem during our first home game of 2017. It was Cliff and I and young Frank. It meant so much to me, not just to have his support but also because it shows he is growing. I hope people give him the chance to show the person he's becoming.

The 12s will also always be my family. For those who don't know, that's the nickname of the Seattle fan base. We may not agree on every issue, but you don't agree with your family on everything. Seattle fans are some of the most famous in this sport for a reason. Their passion and their ability to hit record noise decibels when the other team's offense is on the field are without compare. I once joked that the Seahawks are so popular in Seattle that "Russell Wilson got pulled over and the cop got a ticket."

Let's be honest—being a fan is its own kind of thing. The ego of an athlete can quickly get it twisted. They aren't fans of you the person. They're fans of the way you hit the QB, catch the ball, or run and jump, and that's fine. They're fans of your uniform or the city you represent. But a fan is also someone we can reach. If they hear about the work we do off the field, maybe they won't care. Or maybe they'll see the hope we can bring to a poverty-stricken area, a prison, or our hometown, and maybe they'll come out of their shell, and we can be more than just people who wear the same colors. I've seen it: the transformation of people in the 12s from being fans to feeling inspired. They start to look at you and root for you in a different way. It's a different feeling. I love the 12s, and I feel a special connection to those who took that journey with me.

None of this brotherhood could have developed without our coach, Pete Carroll, the man who gets younger every year. Coach Carroll is one of the few NFL coaches who are comfortable letting people be who they want to be. Everyone on the team also knew that when Coach Carroll was the big cheese at the University of Southern California, a private college in South Central Los Angeles, he didn't hang out in the ivory tower. He went into Compton and Crenshaw to speak with players who were dealing with gang issues and lives that were torn apart, not just to recruit them for his team but as mentoring work. So when Pete Carroll walks into an African American family's home and tells a player's parents, "I'm going to take care of your son," and means what he says, it builds up a lot of trust. He understands that people are individuals. A lot of coaches in the NFL, and coaches in general, want players to reflect their own ego. A coach who's uptight and stressed out wants his players to be as anxious and unhappy as he is. But Pete is the opposite: his open-mindedness has let people be their true selves. We had a locker room full of characters. Pete opened up the door for them to speak their minds, and it let them grow into men.

Our brotherhood was earned the hard way. It came from winning the Super Bowl against Denver in 2014 and then losing against New England the next year. We had our scars, and we wore them like medals. We collaborated to inspire each other, and we supported each other even when we disagreed. Collaboration and solidarity are so important when you're trying to change things. This came together for us in a whole new way when Kaepernick first took that knee in August 2016.

After Kaepernick made his stand, I spoke to him on the phone, along with thirty or forty other players on the line, to discuss what we could do to offer support. People were arguing, and it was chaos. Finally, I said to everybody, "Do what you feel is right. It doesn't have to be taking a knee. It could be doing a backflip. We don't all have to agree on the idea of what we need to do, but we all have to agree on the message. The message needs to be that there are a lot of racial injustices going on in America. However you want to make a stance, be like Nike and just do it. And as long as that message goes out to everybody, it will be great." But the media focused more on who was or wasn't taking a knee than on the message. That's propaganda and the disinformation machine at its finest.

In the Seahawks locker room, we did something before opening day that I bet few teams did. Pete Carroll brought us together and we talked for hours about the issues animating Colin's move. We decided, as a team, to link arms before the opening game of the season, held on the explosively patriotic fifteenth anniversary of the 9/11 attacks. The NFL had all kinds of military tributes planned for that day, and even though Colin's protest—all together now, for the thousandth time—had nothing to do with the military, it was a dicey atmosphere for planning an action. Some people criticized us for linking arms during the anthem, saying we should have done nothing but put our hands on our hearts. Other people were critical from the opposite perspective, angry that we didn't all take a knee or burn a jersey at the fifty-yard line, because we were the big, bad, outspoken Seahawks. But not every player is out there and political, and we agreed to do something that we could all buy into. Like I told the media afterward, I've got three kids, and if I ask what they want to eat for dinner, they are all going to say something different. It's hard to get people to agree on a plan, and at the end of that emotional, hours-long meeting, when we all agreed to link arms, I felt like it was a big deal for us to come together—Black players, white players—and connect on one gesture. We wanted to do something symbolic of bringing the community together, and that's what we did.

Linking arms also was a good organizing principle. It allowed us to involve the widest layer of people on the team. Instead of just a couple of us taking a knee, we wanted to expand it. The criticisms afterward, especially from people who supported Kaepernick, were hard to hear, and, in my view, they also aided the people who wanted to shut us up and shut us down. I believe that you have to meet people where they are at, and the easiest way to disable a whole bunch of folks is to turn them against each other. That didn't happen. Our goal was to plant the seeds in the locker room and in these communities where we work and are seen as role models. We also wanted to pose an all-important question to everyone, not just players: "If you are concerned about these issues, what's next? What are you prepared to do?"

The message didn't get out there as much as I wanted, but for me, linking arms was a way to say, "If we're going to talk it, we've got to live it, and the hardest thing for people to do is to live it. We want to protest. We also want to set an example as being the kind of people who take care of our families and our community; the kind of people who don't do commercials with McDonald's, poisoning kids; the kind of people who do more than tweet hashtags when a sister or brother is killed."

My man Steve Hauschka was a vital voice in this meeting, telling white players that we needed to make a stand together. It took hours, and I mean hours, to talk it through as an entire locker room. People had tears in their eyes and were getting choked up while talking. It made me realize that when it's all said and done, no matter who we are and no matter what we achieve on the field, we all feel one another's pain. That's when I felt that brotherhood cement itself, and I'll tell you, it was one of the greatest feelings of my life. It was better than winning the Super Bowl. There was something about that meeting and the way we opened up to each other that I will never forget. You sit next to a person for four or five years and think you know them. Then it gets real and you say, "Wow, I never knew you felt like that. Dang, we really are brothers."

I also felt I was seeing the possibility for men to evolve in this country, and not to hold anything inside. It's tough to imagine a more macho atmosphere than an NFL locker room. Nobody ever wants to be emotional, unless it's getting emotional about winning the next game and kicking butt. It's easier, always, to be hard than to be vulnerable. But when I saw teammates of mine, who could knock someone into next week between the lines, shedding a tear when they talked about the world outside the NFL bubble, it really changed my mind-set.

Of course we had our cliques. It's a big locker room, and you're drawn to people who think like you, dress like you, come from the same part of the country as you. It's like, "Okay, I don't know anybody here, but you're from Texas, so we got something in common." But the core that defined this team was the slowly expanding group of us that is socially minded. We understand that we are living in a defining moment. We are at a crossroads when it comes to our young people, their lives, the food they eat, the air they breathe, and the kinds of lives they are going to lead. We understand that because of technology and social media, we can play a role in shaping this future. Ten of us in a room can reach fifty million people. That's power, and we take it seriously. We also know that this is why the big sports media networks, as well as the NFL, police and scrutinize our platform so hard. They want us to be brands, not men. They want us to keep it to sports—and I get it. It's not us buying the season tickets or the luxury boxes, but at the end of the day, we're human beings. We're not just equipment.

My friends on other teams, they would say, "Man, what are you guys doing? You are crazy! We could never do that here." I'm talking about the best players in this league: top-ten players going to the Hall of Fame. They feel constricted, yet they are the ones with the *most* job security. They loved that we could be ourselves. For the majority of NFL players, the only time they really act like themselves is when they're at home. They can dance and sing in the shower and shimmy with a Hula-Hoop, with Al Green playing. They would see us and ask, "How is Michael Bennett saying whatever he wants to say? I want to do the same thing." But more players could be themselves if they just tried. It's like that expression, "You don't know you're chained until you try to move."

When I was traded to the Eagles, I knew there would be no guarantee of a brotherhood. We fought for this as a team. We fought to be a political statement of a different way for a team to operate, and a break from the NFL macho "shut up and play" code of self-destruction. This Seattle team taught me that sports don't have to be toxic. They can be a force for good. What makes sports toxic so often is the greater society, which puts people on pedestals and lets people—from star athletes to Hollywood executives to presidents—get away with toxic behavior.

The essence of sports is beautiful: people coming together to achieve a goal regardless of their color, race, or religion. Everything about that sounds beautiful. It sounds like a healthy marriage. It sounds like commitment. It sounds like dedication. It sounds like passion. It sounds like everything worth rising out of bed for. But it gets destroyed by society, by valuing wealth over play; by professionalizing sports for our kids, which sets them against each other even when they are on the same team; by having locker rooms where people can't be themselves; by caring about winning more than the process of how you get there. The glorification of those kinds of values is what makes sports toxic. I believe that sports has a role in changing society, from youth leagues to the pros. If nothing else, sports offers us a platform, both culturally and financially, to try to effect the kind of change that can transform entire communities and even shake up the world.

WITHOUT FOOD, YOU'RE GOING TO DIE

Service to others is the rent you pay for your room here on earth.

—**Muhammad Ali**

I love to eat. But I don't live to eat. I eat to live. This issue of food and what is known as "food justice" has been a journey for me, from growing up spending summers on a Louisiana farm, eating only healthy foods straight out of the earth that I picked with my own hands, to going through a long period where nothing I ate was healthy. Everything was processed: the quicker and greasier, the better. Then in the NFL I started to take nutrition seriously, and my performance on the field changed. But it was important to much more in my life than football. Eating with a healthy mind-set changed my sleep, my state of mind, and even my skin.

I've moved from just thinking about eating healthily to seeing food as an issue that demands activism. It didn't happen by accident. I was invited to a government forum on the problem of childhood obesity in in the United States. This was a life-changing experience, although probably not in the way the organizers of this event wanted it to be. The childhood obesity forum brought together people from different areas to address this pressing issue. There were political officials, nutritionists, and school superintendents on the scene, but there were also representatives from McDonald's, Coca-Cola, and Pepsi. I was sitting there, listening, taking it all in—and slowly I started to get furious. The people from McDonald's, Coke, and Pepsi were talking about kids as the source of the problem, as if kids were stupid for choosing to consume the companies' products: the nasty crap they push kids to eat and drink. I was thinking, *They are talking about me. If I were still a kid, I would be the very stereotype they are branding as the source of the problem of this national health crisis.*

Imagine the nerve: here's McDonald's and Coca-Cola talking about how they want to help these kids to not be a problem. I'm thinking, *You guys are the problem! How are you even here at a roundtable to discuss nutrition? Who let you in?!?* I had to speak right then and there. I started chewing them out in that room. I said, "What you guys are saying is not true! If given the opportunity and the right resources, these kids would eat right. I don't care what y'all are saying. They drink sixty-four-ounce cups of soda because this is what they have, and what you guys are pushing on them."

That day I was so mad, I decided to start my foundation. I went straight home to Pele and said, "Did you know this is going on? The people sitting in a room making decisions about childhood nutrition are the ones who benefit from obesity." That's why my foundation deals with every aspect of food, from the earth to the plate. I do it because it needs to be done.

I feel like I'm on a mission to share how food can be a tool for personal and community liberation with people who don't get to hear this kind of talk; people who don't learn about nutrition in school, at home, or in daily life; people who are never taught how veggies can help prevent disease or how a balanced meal can make the difference as to whether kids can concentrate in school. Our ancestors knew what type of food to prepare when people were sick or needed comfort. They used specific foods at certain times of the year to fortify immune system defenses. We have forgotten these lessons—or they have been stamped out of our heads by processed food giants—at the cost of our health and our happiness.

We've got goals for our foundation. Big picture, I want to end food deserts. Not desserts. Not sweets. Deserts. The definition of a desert is land that is "usually waterless and without vegetation." If you've ever lived in a food desert, you know what they are without my having to explain it to you. A food desert is an entire neighborhood, a place segregated by poverty and race, with nowhere to find cheap and healthy food. Food deserts are when adequate nutrition is absent in your community and you need a car to get to a real grocery store. It's when the closest thing to fresh produce is Cheeto-dusted pork rinds. It's when food is fast food and ordering off the McDonald's dollar menu on your corner makes more sense than five dollars in bus fare and an hour in traffic just to get to a quality supermarket. It's when a liquor store with a spinning bulletproof-glass cash register to pay for cigarettes and Skittles is your version of Whole Foods.

When you eat that way, it doesn't just slow you down. It makes you not want to live. There are too many communities like this, and if you are not eating properly, forget about after-school programs. Forget about learning at all. Ask a room of poor kids how many have eaten fast food five times that week. Then ask how many in their families have colon cancer or diabetes. You'll see a roomful of hands go high after both questions.

More than money, more than cars, more than shoes, it's food that's the essence of everything in your body. Without food, you're going to die. If you don't have a piece of protein and a plate of veggies when you need some protein and veggies, that's your death sentence. It's a twenty-first-century version of oppression—it's new, and we haven't figured out how to discuss it or break the conversation as wide open as it needs to be. Even during slavery, we may have been getting beaten, but we were better nourished back then because everything we ate was grown in front of us, even if it was the scraps. The soil was rich. The nutrients were plentiful. The toxic element was the slave system itself. We were brought here from the African continent, where we cooked what we grew. Now, everything we eat is processed, and it's killing us. So many kids have problems with their weight that didn't exist fifty years ago. I've seen kids four or five years old with diabetes, weighing a hundred pounds. I've seen kids who don't have the energy to play video games, let alone sports.

The numbers will scare you. According to the Centers for Disease Control and Prevention, obesity affects 17 percent of all US children. That's 12.7 million of our young people. Race and racism impact these numbers: obesity affects 22 percent of Latinx children and 19 percent of non-Latinx Black children.

How did we get to this point? It's chilling when you talk to a child and they don't even know what a vegetable is. They have never seen an onion or even heard the word, and they think French fries are a vegetable. One kid we were working with thought a darn strawberry was a small apple. It wasn't his fault, but I'm like, *What? What school are you going to?* Food is so important—and that's why I focus my foundation work on nutrition and how food creates the preconditions for a healthy body and mind. But we have so far to go. If food is self-determination, then right now, that self-determination does not exist.

Athletes have a moral responsibility to step up and do something about this, because we have been lying to children for years. We sell junk food to kids who look like us. We pretend we eat this and imply that this is how we were able to rise to the top of our sports. We say, "Hi, kids! I eat McDonald's!" But Michael Jordan is not eating McDonald's. He has a chef. I guarantee that Jordan spends a million dollars a year on his food, and it's not a million dollars of Big Macs.

We need to stop selling this poison, and we need to end the food deserts in poor areas. The people who run Whole

Foods don't want to build stores in these neighborhoods, unless they are neighborhoods "in transition," where poor people of color are going to be forced out anyway. They say it's not profitable to build in these communities, and they can't or won't drop their prices to make food affordable. This is why Pele and I are committed to building a network of community gardens and, once we have set them up, killing the myth that eating healthy is so expensive you couldn't do it.

Food education means the world to me: giving people the opportunity to understand how nutrition plays a key role in being healthy, intelligent, and able to live your best life. We say to families, "We know how tough it is out there to make a food budget work. But let us work with you. You buy five Happy Meals and four burgers, it's twenty-seven dollars, right? Let's talk about how to go to the grocery store and shop for a twenty-seven-dollar healthy meal. Or fifteen dollars? Twelve dollars? Let's talk about how we can try to make it work." But it's often a deeper problem than how to grocery shop, though. Often, the parents we speak to just don't have the time to cook or are too exhausted from work. The commute to the nearest supermarket with fresh produce is also a killer. We do cooking demonstrations to show how to make preparing food as time-effective as possible, but we know we are up against a lot of real-life obstacles as we move forward.

This passion for food justice is why I partnered with the Freedom School in Seattle. It's a summer program based on the original Freedom Schools in the South during the civil rights movement. The Freedom Schools believed that literacy, history, and life are best learned through struggle, and this school is part of that tradition. At the Seattle Freedom School, kids learn about the history of struggles for justice, then they pick a project they want to focus on, and the whole summer culminates in their day of action. In 2017, they picked food justice. Their action was a march and rally, leading up to speakouts in front of all the fast food restaurants near their school. They talked about nutrition, the lack of healthy food in communities of color, and the lack of a living wage for the restaurant workers. I brought the Freedom School to the Seahawks preseason camp. The kids looked at us like we were heroes, but I wanted as many of my teammates as possible to meet with these amazing young people and learn something from them.

Pele and I, with our foundation, also do food justice work in youth prisons. If you go to what they call "a juvenile detention center" and ask a counselor who's been there for twenty years what the difference is between kids today and back when the counselor started, they'll say that it's not that youth prisoners are more dangerous or more violent now. It's that they are more tired. The word used is "lethargic." They don't want to play sports. They don't want to move. It's the coming together of depression and junk food, but it's bigger than just having no energy. These kids don't want to live. If you don't eat healthily, you don't want to be alive. I've built community gardens inside these detention centers, teaching kids how to garden, and you would be surprised how these young people—demonized as super-predators but too defeated on some days to get out bed—come to life. One kid told me something I'll never forget. He said, "This project is not only teaching me what to eat, but it's showing me that I'm a human being. When I eat something that I grow, I feel like I am not in jail anymore."

Outside the prison system, when I meet kids who do eat healthily, the whole family is doing the work and taking the time to help them learn the basics of nutrition. Think about the Black Panther Party in the 1960s and 1970s—one of their central focuses was on food and breakfast programs. This wasn't just for the purpose of helping the community survive. It was to pressure the government to initiate more breakfast and lunch programs to provide healthy food to schoolkids. We need that pressure now, not just because the president wants to end the school breakfast programs we still have, but because the breakfasts that are currently provided are garbage. Let's make real food for our kids instead of garbage on a paper plate. Get rid of these Jimmy Dean sausages with French toast wrapped around them and syrup for dipping. Give our kids real food! Teach our kids the importance of eating healthily. Give our kids the chance to not be obese.

The Department of Education says, "Look. These kids get a veggie, a starch, and some protein. What's the problem?" The problem is that it is all out of a can. You go to a wealthy private school, and the kids are on line at the salad bar. It's an old joke, but at too many public schools the only thing green to eat is the meat loaf. As much as the Department of Education spends on standardized testing, they could spend some of that money on fresh food and give these kids a chance.

You go to countries like Finland or Japan, and eating to live instead of living to eat is a way of life. Food is essential to everything they do: the hub of the wheel in their lives. I was in Japan for the first time in 2016, and there, food is everything. They take it as seriously as we take the NFL. In schools, lunch is a class. And that's not unique to Japan. In many places around the world, lunch is a class where kids learn how to cook, how to clean, and how to eat properly. As Michael Moore showed in his movie *Where to Invade Next,* when you give kids in other countries our school lunches, they start to cry. I couldn't believe that scene. The kids were actually crying, asking, "What are you trying to do to us?"

Why are public school lunches so terrible? A lot of big brands are invested in school "nutrition," so they give schools access to their products in order to reach kids at a young age. We need a return to when schools had cooks making meals fresh in the back. Make the food fatty and delicious as long as it's not processed, and as long as the plate has five different natural colors. That means veggies. That means fruit. That means life.

Good food is the foundation not just for a healthy body but for a ready mind. It sets the mind up for learning. And to feed the mind, we need more STEM education—science, technology, engineering, and math—especially geared toward young girls. It's something I dream about, imagining if kids were as focused on STEM as they are on sports. Our goal is to fund and set up STEM programs all over the world for two reasons. First, when kids are taught these subjects correctly—hands-on teaching, experiments, kids doing physical projects—their brains light up, because it speaks to their creativity. It's learning by doing. Second, STEM opens doors to economic opportunity. Before Dr. King was killed, he was exploring the question of economic justice, asking, "What's the point of being able to sit at a lunch counter if you cannot afford a cup of coffee?" This is my way of trying to carry on his work from a different angle.

In this country, if you have money, people treat you like a human being. If you don't have money, they treat you like dirt. That's life. If you don't have money, it's almost impossible to eat well. If you have resources, you can eat in a way that feeds your body and mind. If young people are educated in STEM, it gives them a much greater opportunity for freedom than throwing a football. To have knowledge in a STEM field means having a seat at the table of the future, because the future is technology, and if you're not helping to create that technology—from communications to space exploration to environmental management—then you're just cutting yourself off. It is crucial to be part of the creating process. For Black people, this is where our history becomes connected to economics. We need to understand our history as creators. Yes, we want you to stop calling us n----rs. Yes, we want you to stop locking us up. But when I teach Black history in my kids' classes and talk to them about the inventions that Black people have contributed to our society—from the refrigerated truck to the traffic light—it shocks the students, because they didn't know. If you are empowered and excited by this history, it seems more realistic that you can get a seat at the table, do it yourself, and be a part of the future. Sports is a dead end because there is no ownership potential. Playing this game has given me a platform and money to educate my kids. But STEM education gives my daughters a chance to create and own.

To me these twin issues, food justice and STEM education, are key if we are going to see the next generation climb out of poverty, and I want to be a part of building that ladder. I'd never thought about these issues on a global scale until I traveled to Haiti with my teammate and brother, Cliff Avril. Cliff's been doing work and supporting his parents' home country for years. In 2017, I went with him, and what I saw has had a searing effect on me, like a scar I notice every time I look in a mirror. I saw pain and suffering that hurt me in a way no offensive lineman ever could. It reminded me of being young and asking my mother, "Why?" As in, *Why does the world even have to be like this?* If you don't ask why, you'll never be attacked or criticized. No one is going to go after you or your family. But if you don't ask why, nothing, not a single thing, is ever going to change. I think that's the difference between philanthropy and activism. Philanthropy is this kind of life-saving work. Activism is when you ask why this work needs to be done in the first place. Cliff Avril does both because he's got the soul of an activist.

I grew up with an idea of Haiti as almost a fairyland for Black folks: a place founded by a victorious slave rebellion. I assumed Haiti was the Super Bowl of Black freedom, like Atlanta on steroids. I thought, before seeing it for myself, that while there would be poverty, I was going to see Black industry, Black scientists, Black teachers, and a Black world running with inspiring beauty. Instead, I saw devastation. I saw people who could have been my cousins—and with the slave trade, you never know—living in a state of pain in a country still wrecked from the 2010 earthquake. I saw destruction and disarray, but I also saw beautiful people, loving each other and hustling. The pain messed up my mind. It was depressing to see so many people without access to education, clean water, or hospitals. It was also humbling to see the drive that people had to live their lives, rebuild, and not be bitter at everyone and everything.

Through Cliff's guidance, I also learned something about resilience. I met kids who were walking miles just to go to school and parents working for less than a dollar a day. I worked in an orphanage in Port-au-Prince that Cliff supports, and the workers there told me about people who, with tears in their eyes, would drop kids off at the orphanages because they couldn't afford to raise them. These families would say, "If I keep this baby, they will starve. This is their only chance at survival." We got to work feeding the kids: the food was rice and some chicken. When I was feeding these kind, polite young people, I saw that they had bowls for the rice but very few spoons. I saw them then share spoons so they could eat it. But what I'll never forget is how much pride they took in what they ate. They calmly waited turns to use those spoons, even though they were starving, so they could eat with dignity. I also spoke to a woman who worked at a hospital; she told me they can only take in six women giving birth in a day, so if a seventh woman comes, she has to give birth outside.

These were people on the edge of survival, but they still kept fighting. I met children who walked miles and risked drowning as they crossed a rickety bridge, just to get to school. They did it not only for knowledge but also because school was where they were going to get their one meal that day. This is a school Cliff is rebuilding, in a community called Le Charme. It's about ninety minutes from the airport, but with Haiti's lack of paved roads, it took us almost four hours to get there. Cliff is taking this school that looks like it could barely stand up to a stiff wind, with bedsheets hung up to create separate rooms, and turning it into a real school, with six classrooms, completely hurricane- and earthquake-proofed.

Seeing the kids light up at the idea that their school—and therefore their future—had a chance led me to imagine what could happen if they had any kind of financial support. They would work hard and contribute to the world in ways we cannot foresee. But nobody is investing in Haiti. Maybe it's still to punish them for their revolution in 1804. Maybe if there were gold or oil under the ground, people would figure out a way to care.

The Haitian people were incredibly kind to us and loved that we were there. It's not like they knew us from *NFL Sunday Ticket* or were Seahawks fans. I think it was more that they saw Black people coming to provide aid and Black people with some resources, so there was a sense of trust. They wanted to know who we were. In us, they saw hope.

Haiti inspired me because its people inspired me. I saw people in conditions you can't imagine, still trying to make better lives for themselves and their families. I will never abide anybody calling Haiti a s---hole, like President Trump did.

It also gave me the perspective that so much of what we think really matters, doesn't. At the core of everything is survival, and it pushes you to ask questions until you get answers: *Why don't people in Haiti have access to clean water? Why don't people have books? Why don't they have medicine? Why can't they have bathrooms that work?* It blows your mind. It's not like Haiti is poor because it has no resources. This place was called the Jewel of the Antilles because enough wealth was taken from its earth to enrich the entire continent of Europe. All this money was made off of Haiti, but when the people of Haiti freed themselves from France in 1804, the French charged Haiti to pay them back because France had "lost its property." Haiti is still paying off debt to France. I wouldn't pay them anything. *What are you going to take? You took everything, there ain't nothing left!*

There's trash everywhere. There are still crushed buildings every place you look. There are people who still don't know if their loved ones died in the earthquake, and it was eight years ago! It's easy to question all of humanity when you see Haiti. But the trip also left me thinking about my friend Cliff, and I was like, *Wow, what he's doing is so much bigger than anything I've thought about.* A lot of players in the NFL do foundation work. Some are passionate about it; for others it's just PR or a tax shelter. But either way, whatever the work we do, how much of an impact are we making? Are we saving lives?

Having seen a lot of poverty in the United States, I'd say that the difference between here and Haiti is that the opportunity for a better life in Haiti seems so much more narrow. But there are parts of the United States where conditions are similar; we just choose not to see them. Last year I went to South Dakota to run a football and health clinic for the Lakota Sioux tribe. As in Haiti, I saw poverty, pain, and no investment. But also as in Haiti, I saw resilience, a culture of family, and a deep belief in the power of spirituality. It's humbling to see that kind of resilience and spirit alongside the loss they have suffered and continue to suffer. The past isn't past for the Sioux. The people I was with are fifty minutes away from any access to fresh food. They live on the Badlands, which is literally bad land: land that can barely grow crops. These people have an incredibly close relationship with the earth, yet their lives are built around processed foods. I saw dangerously overweight kids. It was impossible to avoid the contrast: poverty and malnutrition in Haiti mean starvation, while poverty and malnutrition here mean early-onset diabetes and obesity.

It's also near impossible for them to find banks to deposit their money. They are isolated from every potential lifeline to hope, but their fighting spirit remains. The Sioux spoke to me about the confidence they feel from the fight against the Dakota Access Pipeline at Standing Rock. It was a movement to keep their earth unpolluted, and they faced down tanks and teargas to do it. Win or lose that fight, the confidence they gained from waging it isn't going away anytime soon.

I see all this pain, and strength in the face of it, and I wrestle with how to increase my philanthropy and also build the bridge I described, between philanthropy and activism. I've announced that every endorsement I get will now go to charity, specifically channeled into underserved communities of color. I didn't go public with this for extra attention. I wanted to spotlight it as a way to encourage the companies that want me to endorse their products to match what I'm doing. This has been far more difficult to accomplish than I thought it would be. I've sat across the table from company reps to talk about improving what they give back, and they look at me like they're malfunctioning robots, saying, "Does not compute." It has shown me that even companies that talk a good game aren't really invested in communities. Too many will do just enough for public relations and then shut the door. The only difference between them and Enron is smarter accountants.

The goal is to pressure companies to make them accountable for how they operate, and how they profit, in our communities. You look at some of the grocery stores and businesses in Black neighborhoods. You look at what Chris Rock calls "the Black mall" and compare it to "the white mall," and you see the gap. As Rock says, "There ain't nothing in the Black mall. Nothing in the Black mall but sneakers and baby clothes."

Much of that is because a lot of white communities have a business association to invest in their neighborhoods, parks, and infrastructure. Look at a suburban kids' football team, and that team has ten logos all over the uniforms. When you look at Black communities, it's different. All the screaming faces on cable news were so critical of the people in Ferguson for "tearing down their community"—when in reality it's not truly their community, because most of the businesses aren't community owned, and the businesses that are there don't give back. They are taking money out of the community. They're extracting the wealth, little different from the situation in Haiti. It's the private business version of the police writing up excessive parking tickets in Ferguson.

As athletes, we have a tremendous untapped power to hold accountable the Fortune 500 companies that sign us to endorsements. Instead of our signing nine-figure deals with Nike, imagine if we started from the point that Nike owes our community money: a $200 million trust aimed at—to use just one example—eliminating food deserts in the United States, and then we work with them on administering it. If athletes came together to demand these kinds of investments in exchange for our sponsorship, it would make all the difference in the world. I think about the number of community gardens that could be thriving with that kind of investment.

The problem is that we might be the face of Nike or Adidas, but we have no control, and don't try to have control, over the direction of the company beyond what colors or design we want on our products. We are just an extension of the Nike brand.

That's why it makes me so uncomfortable when people on the business and accounting side of my life ask, "How are you building your personal brand?" It rings so ugly in my ears because a brand is a product. A brand is a thing. A brand is something to be sold. It tries to define who a person is by what they are selling. The brand becomes a symbol in their mind of who you are, leasing out your integrity so it is associated with their product. You are supposed to get some shine from their image as well, like, "Oooh! That person is a Nike guy." But sneaker companies make their shoes in China, pay low wages, and then lie about how people there are lucky to make a dollar a day. There is no integrity in that. But if a player challenges the limits of being a brand—say, by protesting during the anthem—then the brand will drop them with a quickness. Sneaker companies are like the evangelical preachers who condemn all the "sinners" while kissing Trump's behind.

This language of speaking about athletes as a brand also muzzles them. It covers up their mouths. Your advisors, agents, or managers will whisper in your ear, "Don't say that! It's going to hurt your brand!" That "brand" of being an athlete means "staying in your lane" and smiling for the camera. It means "shut up and dribble." It means never being allowed to pursue alternative ideas about who you really are because you have been kept in an athletic vacuum. You have been told that success doesn't come from education or study or the discovery of a new path, but from rejecting these things for a hyperfocus on football. A lot of people stay in this vacuum, and there's no growth. I've seen it. Players in the locker room saying, "Why do I need to grow? People tell me how to eat, what to wear, and how to think, and my bank account is flush. I'm good!" But there is spiritual death at the end of that journey. It's why athletes have a hard time dealing with themselves after retirement—because they don't know who they are. They don't know what food they like. They don't know what their hobbies are. They don't even know what color they like. They've played for a team that wears blue and green, and guess what? Their favorite colors are blue and green. Too many of us are like child actors who only grow up when we retire. Then we're just a bunch of full-grown Gary

Colemans (may he rest in peace). We have a brand that's been created by Twitter, a management team, or the media. There is never that point of reflection, to ask, "Hey, what do I believe in? What gives me joy?"

They don't think about developing their minds and obsess over their bodies, but it's hard to put the blame on athletes, because that's our obsession as a society. We praise the running, the jumping, and the showcase muscles, but we respond harshly when they think outside the box or speak controversial ideas. We don't like them to focus on hobbies, because once an athlete starts exploring quirky, fun interests outside of football, the questions start: "Why isn't he focusing on his sport? Why is Martellus Bennett writing children's books and developing an entire animated series? He dropped three passes last year. Can he focus on catching those three passes? Why is Michael Bennett in Africa, taking a STEM program to Senegal? When is he going to have time to do his weight lifting?"

If you're not doing what people think you should be doing, which is focusing on football and selling products, you are seen as a misfit. You are seen as different. You are seen as unconventional because you are using what you see as your platform in a way that isn't just about getting everyone paid.

I mentioned the Muhammad Ali quote that speaks to this earlier, to describe Russell Wilson. Ali was asked why he had to speak out on racism and war, and he said, "I don't have to be who you want me to be." Everybody wants you to be who they want you to be, but then you're not you anymore. I try to offer a counterexample to being that person who wears the mask and just says, "Well, we play one game at a time, good lord willing." If a game was bad, I'll say, "The game was bad." After we lost to the Falcons in the 2016 playoffs, I said to a reporter, "Get out of my face now. Don't tell me I didn't do my job. I just put my heart on that field. Don't play with me." I regretted losing my temper, but I didn't regret not wearing the mask. That's just me. I apologized to the reporter later because that's me, too.

In the same way, if I don't like something that's going on in society, I'll let you know or I'll try to do something about it. That's not just how you find your voice. It's how you keep from losing your mind. It's easy to lose your life quickly or in slow motion, if you look in the mirror every single day and don't know who you are.

Martellus once said to me that getting out of Texas was the best thing that ever happened to him, because in Texas people would only let him be a football player. He was a star in high school and college and then ended up on the Cowboys. People think that must've been a dream come true, but the truth is that being in Dallas kept him in a box. The Dallas Cowboys got mad at him because he was investing time in his creative pursuits. Rob Gronkowski could go out act like a fool and be at WrestleMania, and that was okay because it's "on brand," but if you try to create they'll say you're not focused.

But Martellus is exceptional on every level. If you're a more typical player, you don't know what to say or think unless someone tells you. You know you're big and strong, but at the end of the day that's a mask. Inside, you're just as emotional as the next person. You can have everything in the world, but if you're not attached to your emotions, you have no inner being. You're just a shell. The journey is about going from being a shell to being yourself. That's the hardest thing to do for an athlete because it comes with a cost. That cost is, "If I don't fall in line the way they want me to, I'm not going to have a Nike commercial. I'm not going to be the face of an airline. I'm not going to be the face of anything. I judge myself not by my family or loved ones. I judge myself by the power of my brand."

We become this way because for much of the time, when we are out of uniform and trying to develop this holy "brand," we are dealing with parasites. There are a lot of fine agents and managers out there, but by definition they all are connected to you not by love or a shared sense of mission, but by the equation, "If he don't get paid then I don't get paid." You're dealing with parasites at all times. It creates the hardest challenge in sports: How do I defy all odds and be myself? How do I take the Dave Chappelle approach? The public says they want celebrities to be about something more than the money, but they called Chappelle "crazy" because he dared to live it. There are so few models to work from, unless you are talking about the wealthiest people in the world, people so rich they can be whoever they want to be and always have a crowd ready to applaud. In Seattle, I see Bill Gates being a philanthropist, and no one says, "Stop giving money to fight cancer! You don't even have cancer!" Or, "You're too rich to worry about poverty. This is a distraction from creating the new smartphone! Why are you trying to solve a problem you don't face?"

My family worries that my approach will eventually leave me with nothing: no team, no sponsors, no partners. That's the first thing my Uncle Jerry tells me when he calls. He says, "Michael, do you know what? I love you and I love what you're doing, but you have to stay on the straight line, simply because they're waiting for you to fall. They're waiting for you to make 'a n---a mistake.' And as soon as you make 'a n---a mistake,' they're going to tear everything down that you're speaking on. No matter how much good you do."

It's a lot of pressure. But Uncle Jerry starts with the vinegar and ends with the honey, saying, "Michael, I know that you are who you are, so continue to do what you do. But don't put yourself in bad situations where they can come back and tear you down, because there are so many people looking at you for inspiration, whether you believe it or not."

I didn't believe it until I heard from my grandma, who lives in a small town. She told me, "Every time I go to the grocery store, they're talking about what you're doing. So you're affecting a lot of different people. You just got to stay on the straight road." That last part is a tough truth. As a Black man in public view, the margin for error is next to nothing. If I were a white man, I could make a mistake. You can be someone who brags about sexually assaulting women *on videotape* like Trump and still become the president. I can't drink and drive—not that I would. I can't be riding around with guns. I cannot do any of those things. Not only because it would it gut my family. It would define me forever. No matter how much work I do, no matter the message, I'd be discredited. Everything I have ever done, every bit of the work with the foundation, with food,

with STEM programs, would be discredited if not destroyed. It's a test. But I like tests like that. I have to walk the talk. I have to transcend the human temptation to do things to blow up my life.

It's okay, though. I'm focused on being a man of my word, to my community, my teammates, and most important, my family. I'm coaching my daughter's basketball team. I'm teaching at her school. I'm in the community because it's real life and it's filled with small miracles.

But at the end of the day, I'm a Black man. Even though my economic situation has changed, my platform, my substance, my soul is still in my community. When I go back and see kids struggling, I don't know the type of man I'd be if I didn't try to help—not only with resources but with organizing, too, so they can help themselves. That's why Black Lives Matter is not just a slogan or a hashtag to me. It's a call to action. But before we get to why Black Lives Matter, I want to talk about a word that feeds the idea that Black lives are expendable.

"N----R"

Let's start with the definition of what this word means:

1. Slang: Extremely Disparaging and Offensive.

    a. a contemptuous term used to refer to a black person.

    b. a contemptuous term used to refer to a member of any dark-skinned people.

2. Slang: Extremely Disparaging and Offensive.

    a contemptuous term used to refer to a person of any racial or ethnic origin regarded as contemptible, inferior, ignorant, etc.

3. a victim of prejudice similar to that suffered by black people; a person who is economically, politically, or socially disenfranchised.

There was something about seeing Nazis and KKK and Grand Dragons marching in Charlottesville in August 2017 that reminded me and reminded a nation what the word "n----r" is really all about. It's not a hip-hop catchphrase or even a slur that some coward spray-paints on a wall. It's a word of violence. It's a word they say when they raise their torches and rally around statues of slave owners. It's a word that has one aim: to dehumanize us and turn us into something less than a person so we are easier to kill, easier to drag behind a truck, easier to dump into a lake, easier to shoot in the back. That's all it is. It's a word that erodes our humanity, a means to an end, and that end is our death.

I want this word to die just like I want the ideas that lead people to wear swastika bands on their arms to die. And that's why I want to apologize to my ancestors, my family, and especially my daughters for all the times I've used this word thoughtlessly over the course of my existence. I want to apologize for my role in giving the word life. I know it's different when a Black person says it than coming from a white person. The meaning and intent often differ. That's not the point of this apology.

My point is that I now realize the only reason I used it is because I did not realize its impact and its power. I did not fully understand what our people had endured while hearing this word, and I did not understand how there are people in my community and even in my family who hear it and it carves up their insides, especially the older generation, who hear it and think about what was yelled at them when they were on the way to a school they were brave enough to desegregate. We need to stop using it, and this isn't me pointing the finger. I'm looking in the mirror. I need to do better. I've been ignorant, and I'm guilty for saying it, for being a model for other young Black people who say it and—this really stings to admit—I am guilty for making my white friends, when I was younger, feel comfortable saying it, like it's a joke. I'm haunted by the idea that my daughters will say it like it's nothing. This is my guilt because I want to see myself as a leader, yet here I am, giving this word of slavery and violence life when it needs to be buried in the ground.

The first time I remember hearing the word and feeling subhuman was from a white classmate in Louisiana. I was in grade school, and I beat this kid in some kind of meaningless game at recess. I remember he just looked at me, cold, shrugged his shoulders, and said, "It's fine that I lost because you're still a n----r." I didn't even know what it meant—all I knew was that he wasn't supposed to be saying it. I felt the violent impulse to fight, and something as old as the Louisiana swamps echoed deeply inside both of us. He said it to me because he wanted us to get violent, and that is exactly what happened.

After that schoolyard scuffle, I realized the word was something my family and friends said to each other casually. But I had never heard it consciously. It floated in the air and I kept breathing it in, not realizing how toxic it was. I had family in Texas, Louisiana, Alabama, and Mississippi, and when they got together they used it like it was an adjective or a pronoun or even a comma. I would hear my uncle laugh and say something like, "Oh, this n---a's crazy!" It could be filled with affection, as in, "Man, I love that n---a." Or it could be someone rolling their eyes and saying, "N---a, please." Or it could be used in rage, a cousin saying, "Man, if I see that n---a again, I'm going to kill that n---a." It might even be at the dinner table, when you'd hear with love, "N---a, pass the peas."

It was a word we used as a stand-in for emotions we could not otherwise express. The word made you feel something bone-deep, so we used it to make the people around us understand that what we were saying was real and demanded attention. "I'd die for my friend Rio" doesn't convey the necessary emotion or even sound right. But "I'd die for that n---a" does. That's what is so sick about it: we want people to know that we are feeling love or hate; friendship or anger; pleasure or pain; but to make the people closest to us know that we are getting real—getting human—we come back to a word used to make us believe we are less than human. It's the legacy of white supremacy: our ignorance. My ignorance.

I carried that ignorance until I read what the poet Maya Angelou wrote about racial slurs, and her words haunt me. She said, "I believe that words are things. . . . I think they stick on the walls, they go into the upholstery, they go into your clothes, and finally, into your very body." I believe that, too. The word enters your lungs like asbestos dust, eating away at you from the inside.

The only way to get this cancer out of our bodies is if we reckon with the word's history and see it not as a term of endearment that we are somehow reclaiming, but as the word said before James Byrd was dragged from the back of a truck; the word painted on LeBron James's house before the NBA finals in 2017; and the word chanted in Charlottesville by people who want us gone.

If I heard my daughters use it, no matter how casually, no matter if they were just repeating the lyrics from some music, I would be appalled and tell them that's not a word we use in this house. If it were a regular part of the music they listened to, I wouldn't take their music away, but we'd need to have a conversation every single time I heard it. It might make listening to that music a lot less fun.

This thinking is a recent change for me. I've been coaching and doing clinics my entire adult life. But five years ago, when I was coaching a team and heard some of the kids joking and saying it, I would've said, "Whatever. That's normal. That's just how young people talk." I might have even said, "That's just how n---as talk, man!" But now, I think I would have to stop practice and ask them, as a team, the all-important question, "Why? Why are you guys using that word? Especially when you have white teammates around, hearing that word get normalized, taking away its sting." I've really started to recognize the size of the impression you leave on young people who look up to you. There are times I've let it go, after hearing some young people using it with each other. I threw them a look, and they looked back with a shrug that might as well have said, "What do you expect? I'm just a n---a!" And now I just want to reach back in time, shake their shoulders, and say to them, "That's not all you are!"

It needs to stop. A lot of people have lost their lives because of that word, whether we're talking about lynchings or Black people killing other Black people. It can take a conversation and turn it into something savage at the drop of a hat. It's a word that brings the ugliest part of our past into the present. When white people say it, it brings them back to the time when it was right as rain to put Black people in chains and hang them from trees. It brings them back to when it was fine for us to be mistreated or to have nothing close to equal rights. When a white person says it today, with a scowl on their face, it feels like they're punching my ancestors. I want to fight them, but I also just want to plead with them, on behalf of my great-grandparents: "Haven't my ancestors been through enough? Stop, already!"

The word also divides the Black community. We still look at each other like there are house n----rs and field n----rs, without understanding that it's better to be nobody's n----r. There is a scene in the movie *Deep Cover*, where Laurence Fishburne is asked by a white supervisor, "What's the difference between a Black man and a n----r?" Fishburne replies, "The n----r is the one that would even answer that question."

Let us be the generation to drive it out of our vocabulary as a society, but not in a way that's just about banning the word, because that's too easy. Much more difficult is looking honestly at our history. Not just Black history, but ALL of our history. We have a civil rights photo collection in our house, a big, beautiful coffee-table book with images so vivid they cause jaws to drop. When my daughters and their friends pick it up to look at the young Black boys and girls in the middle of a dangerous struggle, I remind them that our eyes are trained to look at the Black faces and their determination as they walk to school. But I tell them also to look at the white faces in the background: the young, jeering faces shouting slurs and throwing things. "All of those folks are now around your granddad's age," I tell my daughters. They're still with us, and those people now walk around, every day, living with what they did, some I'm sure voting for Donald Trump and passing that hatred down to their children's children. That is this country. Them. We cannot afford to pretend they don't live among us.

The NFL announced, to a lot of publicity, that it will be trying to crack down on players who say "n---a" during a game, with refs handing out fifteen-yard penalties for one infraction and an ejection for a second offense. Their reasoning, I think, is rooted more in protecting their brand and policing how Black players talk to one another than in any kind of change. But if it makes some of us think critically and changes some habits, maybe it will be for the best. I think they know that some white fans and white executives and coaches get very uncomfortable with the word. Why does it make them so uncomfortable? That goes less examined. With some of them, I don't necessarily think it's because they hate racism. I think it's because hearing that word reminds them of their own guilt. It reminds them that their ancestors held a savage power over my ancestors. It brings back the time when people stood around a tree to watch a Black man get hanged, while they snacked on popcorn and posed for postcards. Think about watching a hanging as a form of entertainment. Think about how much you would need to dehumanize somebody to be all right with that kind of killing. The word "n----r" is the gateway to a person becoming "strange fruit." It's a word that takes them back. It takes them back to Emmett Till, lynched because they said he whistled at a white woman. But he had a lisp, so it sounded like he whistled but he didn't. He was killed for having a small gap between his teeth, a fourteen-year-old boy, beaten and hanged. I think the savagery of the word reminds them of the time when a lisp could be a death sentence.

The NFL's punishment of Black players for saying "n---a" is also curious, if also ridiculous, if you step back to look at how the word has been used in sports historically. Think about the thousands of white fans who, on July 4, 1910, chanted "Kill the n----r" at the boxer Jack Johnson, when he fought "the Great White Hope," Jim Jeffries. Think about how the word was used against the people we now hold up as the greatest idols of the last one hundred years: people like Joe Louis, Jesse Owens, and Jackie Robinson. At many points they were all subject to crowds that said, "You may be great at sports, but you are nothing but a 'n----r.'" Think about how that behavior from white fans still hasn't died. Adam Jones, of the Baltimore Orioles, had it shouted at him in Boston in 2017, and other Black players came forward to say, "That happens to me in Boston all the time." Pitcher David Price, who plays for the Red Sox, said it happens to him at home. People know that this word will get under somebody's skin, so if you want to provoke a person to act like a barbarian, you say it. You want them "to be that n----r," and saying the word is the first step to turning them into how you see them. Not the way they are at work or with their kids, but your projection of who you want them to be. You get them to be angry. You put them at risk of incarceration. You want them to die, and saying this two-syllable word is step one to getting them on the road to ruin.

We spoke about this issue as a team, on the Seahawks. Coach Carroll brought in Dr. Harry Edwards, the great sports sociologist, to talk with us about the words we're using and

how it affects us. It was a very heated conversation, not the kind of thing you see on *NFL Total Access*. It was one of those "only in Seattle" locker room meetings, where players were pouring their hearts out in an open dialogue. At one point, we realized that we were all trying to say the same thing: we want to see change. How we go about it might be structurally different, it might be emotionally different, but we all want to make this change.

My man Steven Hauschka impressed the heck out of me because he was willing to be vulnerable, turning red and unable to hide his emotions. His face was like a cherry, and I was worried he might stroke out, but still he pressed on. He said, "I don't know what it feels like to be Black. All the white guys here, we can say we think we know this, but we don't. We don't know. But I want to know how I can be a part of the change." He added, "When you grow up in a white neighborhood, you don't really see any Black people. You aren't our neighbors or classmates, so we don't know the struggle. We don't know it." Everybody got so much respect for him because he was genuine and honest. It was like a bridge between all the players arguing. I hated that Hauschka was cut from the team. He's one of my favorite people.

There is an active racist movement in this country. We need to confront it, and so we need to address the history of the word they are shouting. We have to talk about its relevance and discuss how we can change the way that kids regard it, not seeing it as a pronoun or a "filler" word.

It might not have the same meaning when said by a Black person versus a white person, but it has the same effect, even when we say it to each other. Until we recognize that, I think we are going to be lost. At the same time, people who argue that the problem with Black culture is sagging pants, big hair, or calling each other "n---a" are getting it wrong, too. The problems are racism; lack of resources, education, and healthy food; and police brutality. Still, in order to unite to confront these issues, we need to see each other as brothers and sisters—as full human beings—not as "n---as."

As I write this, we are witnessing a mainstreaming of racism and white supremacy. We are seeing more violence on the streets by people with hate in their hearts. We are seeing nooses hung in public places. The mainstreaming of "n----r" is connected to this. One feeds on the other. But none of this is new, and we shouldn't pretend it is. Racists may be more confident now because of who is in the White House, but it's been there all along. There have been lynchings, nooses hanging, and Confederate flags flying for too long. I saw Confederate flags flying at college football games in Mississippi and South Carolina, but because they never really won anything in those years, nobody paid much attention. Confederate symbols are still part of the official Mississippi, Alabama, and Florida state flags. You look back and you're like, "The whole time it's been there? What has been going on? Why haven't we done anything?" We have a chance right now for real change in how we confront racism. The question comes back to morals and spirituality: *Are we going to turn a blind eye, or are we going to confront this living history so we can move forward and make society better for all people?* An example of this was when the former mayor of

New Orleans, a white dude, announced he was going to tear down the statues of slave catchers and racists. He was brave enough to say, "I'm not going to have monuments that are a slap in the face to two-thirds of the city's population."

I saw those young white men, marching at night with torches to keep these monuments up. I want to say to them that just because it's history doesn't make it right. Those monuments stand on top of the blood and backs and genocide of a people. I question whether for them it's really about their history or an excuse to express their hate. We can't be scared. We can't go back. Let's tear these monuments down, along with the word that gives them life. To me this is what Black Lives Matter is all about—a movement to claim our humanity in a country that would deny it.

BLACK LIVES MATTER

I never doubted my ability, but when you hear all
your life, "You're inferior," it makes you wonder if the
other guys have something you've never seen before.
If they do, I'm still looking for it.

—Hank Aaron

On Father's Day 2017, a Seattle resident named Charleena
Lyles called the police because she thought someone was
breaking into her apartment. She lived in transitional housing
for people who formerly had been homeless, and she called
the police to come protect her. Then, a short period after arriving, they took her life. She was shot down in front of three
of her four children. Charleena Lyles was also pregnant.

The police claimed that she was holding two knives and
they feared for their own lives, but in an examination of her
apartment all that was found were kitchen paring knives.
Charleena Lyles also weighed less than one hundred pounds.

The police made no effort to speak to this woman, who allegedly threatened them with something you use to peel an apple. They also didn't try using nonlethal force: no taser, no mace. They just killed her. If you ask me why I say proudly that I consider myself part of the Black Lives Matter movement, and if you still do not understand why I have refused to stand for the anthem, start with Charleena Lyles.

I learned about Charleena's case from Jesse Hagopian, a teacher at Seattle's Garfield High School and a friend of mine. Jesse met Charleena's family at a vigil right after she was killed. He called me and told me about the case. It felt like being punched in the stomach. I asked Jesse if we could set up a meeting with Charleena's brother and sister. I also said that her kids should come. I showed up at Garfield with Pele and Pele's brother Allo, who is a preacher, and we went to Jesse's classroom, arriving a little bit early.

Then the whole Lyles family rolled in. I'm talking cousins and probably like six kids: Charleena's children and a couple of the cousins'. They were still in a daze from what had happened, but anger was beginning to break through the shock. They had just come from the coroner's office, where they learned that Charleena had been killed with seven bullets, four in her back. They couldn't make sense of why this woman, who was so physically tiny, needed to be put down with seven shots in front of her children.

Pele spoke, and at first she broke down crying. Then she pulled it together with the strength I've seen grow inside of her since she was fifteen. She said, "As a mother and as a woman, this really hurts, and I want to make sure that the women of

Seattle stand with Charleena."

I was overwhelmed in the moment, thinking, *There is nothing I can do to make this right, so maybe at least I can make the load of grief on their shoulders just a little less heavy.* We did a prayer circle at the end, standing, with everybody holding hands, all the kids and the family. Pele's brother said a prayer for Charleena. Everybody was in tears.

That's when I said that we needed to do more than pray. We needed to raise money for Charleena's family and have a rally in her name—and that's exactly what we did. In the heat of the summer and without any kind of organizational backing, we put together an event worthy of the woman taken from our city. Three hundred people showed up. Entire families were there. We made sure there was a face-painting tent for the kids and nutritious barbecue for whoever was hungry. We also sold T-shirts I had printed up that said, "I am Charleena Lyles," and then on the back, "#SayHerName." Every dime from every shirt—which we are still selling—goes to her kids.

Charleena Lyles has a huge extended family, so dozens of her people were there. But there were others at the event who had also lost loved ones to police violence. One of the most moving moments, to me, was hearing from a longtime Garfield High School teacher named Janet Dubois, who went public for the first time that day with details about her son being killed by police. It had happened years and years earlier, and she just suffered quietly, never speaking about what took place. I learned later that she had started to tell her story at a Black Lives Matter event at the school, but it was at this rally where she really described what happened. That day helped the people who had endured so much pain feel less alone. Since that time, we hosted the Lyles family at Seahawks training camp, and the team, especially Russ and Cliff, reached out to show them love. That's the brotherhood, right there. Charleena's kids, who had been carrying all this grief, actually looked happy. It was glory.

This is why I support the Black Lives Matter movement: because it helps people realize their worth. People in the movement understand that Black Lives Matter is not just a slogan or a hashtag. It's about resisting the "New Jim Crow," a social system that has created a parallel, separate, and unequal America, defined by mass imprisonment, unemployment, and substandard food and education. Here are some not-so-fun facts, compiled by the *Washington Post*: Black Americans are two and a half times as likely as white Americans to be shot and killed by police officers. We are twice as likely to be unarmed when shot, and three times more likely to be abused while in police custody. Juries give Black defendants sentences that are 20 percent longer than those given to white defendants convicted of the same crimes. We are imprisoned three times as long for the same drug crimes, even though we use drugs, weed included, less than white folks do. And when we get out of jail, a chance for decent employment—or, in some states, even the right to vote—doesn't exist. We are being warehoused in prisons at such a rate that an entire generation has been scarred. In some neighborhoods, it's just women and the elderly and children, with working-age Black men erased from the equation.

This is the "New Jim Crow," and it starts so young it will put tears in your eyes. It begins with the school-to-prison pipeline. Here are some more less-than-fun facts, according to the US Department of Education Office for Civil Rights: 40 percent of all suspended students are Black; 70 percent of in-school arrests happen to Black students; and before you say, "They must have done something to deserve it," consider that Black preschoolers—we are talking about four-year-olds—make up 18 percent of preschoolers yet are almost half of those suspended. (What do you have to do to get suspended from preschool?)

To put it plainly, we have no power because we have no wealth. In greater Boston, as of 2015, the average household wealth—that's the value of everything you own—was $247,500 for whites; $8 for Blacks. That's not a misprint: eight dollars. If that doesn't make you "uncomfortable," if that doesn't make you feel like we need to figure out what our world is doing wrong, you might need to check your pulse.

I also support the Black Lives Matter movement because the idea that white lives matter is a given. We see it from the faces on our money to the faces on Mount Rushmore. White lives matter so much that, as I write these words, there is a bloody fight to take down monuments to slavers who fought the Civil War to keep my people in chains. They are held up as heroes. There are three times as many monuments to Confederates in the US Capitol Building as there are to Black elected officials. If we mattered to this country, how would that even be possible?

It's so important for me to speak out on Black Lives Matter because this movement has the potential to break through the not-caring that this country has developed toward our existence. There are white people, tired of feeling guilty about slavery and racism, who direct that anger at us for fighting for equality instead of directing that anger at their own ancestors. *They* should be the ones tearing down these monuments. But for all of us, it has to go beyond statues. Black lives will matter when we back up the symbolism of tearing down a celebration of our past oppression with a true reckoning of this country's history. I mean, the fact that I don't know my actual honest-to-god last name blows my mind. That's some crazy stuff. Someone could be walking right past me and be my cousin, and I wouldn't even know it. That's how deep rooted this is! Once we start to get to know each other's history—all of our history—it breaks down the walls between us, because we understand that a person might be different from us, but their difference is cool. It's something we can learn from, not something to fear.

We have to fight the numbness. People turn on the TV and see another Black person murdered, and they're like, "What are the Kardashians doing?" We all need to say, "This needs to change." If we can just get a small number of people—a small number of white people and white athletes—to shift from apathy to action, just like my teammate Justin Britt, we can change the world. That's the kind of thinking I try to instill when I talk to kids who aren't Black. Don't feel guilty. Do something to make it better. Help us heal by standing—or sitting—alongside us.

But for Black lives to matter, Black people also need to know our own history. Kids are always surprised when I tell them about all the things that we have designed, written, and created, and it changes their whole perspective. I want them to know that the 3-D special effects technology used in more and more movies today was created by people who look like us. That is a mission for me: to help young people know that we have been more than athletes and entertainers. I try to make sure that I read stories to my girls about African American inventors, historians, and scientists. I need to do it because I've learned, when dealing with the schools my kids attend, that they're not taught these things.

The sports world, I would argue, has a special responsibility to take a stand on Black Lives Matter. I'm for Black Lives Matter because of the memory of athletes past. Jesse Owens won four gold medals in 1936 yet was not invited back to the Olympics as any kind of honored guest until 1968. And he was invited back because the International Olympic Committee wanted him to go into the track and field locker room to tell John Carlos and Tommie Smith not to do anything out on the medal stand. What does it tell you that there was no room for Jesse Owens at the Olympics? It tells me that they didn't care, and that his Black life did not really matter even though he helped define the modern Olympics. People have said to me that, as an athlete, given the money and fame that come with this life, I have no business speaking out. But it's not about me as an individual. If we as a people do not have fairness and equality, then we need to keep standing up, and when that anthem plays I am going to continue to sit. It's like Jackie Robinson said: "People tell me I've got it made because I have fame and some money in my pocket, but I'm concerned with the mass of people." That's my concern as well.

I'm also for Black Lives Matter because, as I said at the start of this book, I'll be a football player for just a few more years, but I'll be Black forever. When I'm driving with my family down the street in a nice car in a nice neighborhood and the police see us, they don't see Michael Bennett the college graduate, the husband, or the loving father. They don't see the Michael Bennett who is wrapped around the fingers of his baby girls. They don't see any of that. They immediately see a Black Man who could possibly be dangerous and possibly be a suspect, and who they should think about pulling over. Many people don't understand that.

My mortality in the face of police violence became a reality for me on the night of August 26, 2017. I had flown to Las Vegas with Cliff to see the Floyd Mayweather–Conor McGregor fight. I am a homebody, and you will rarely see me doing something like this—going to a high-profile fight in Vegas—so, of course, I thought, *I bet something awful happens.* That superstitious vibe was turned up when I saw Sean "Diddy" Combs in the VIP area before the fight. It made me think of Tupac being killed in Las Vegas. It made me think of Biggie Smalls being killed. It made me think about the fact that the FBI found Tom Brady's stolen jersey in Mexico, but they still don't know who killed 'Pac and Big? Thinking about that was like a mosquito in my ear, something I tried to ignore so I could just have some fun.

Before the fight, I sat for the anthem. That's not just for on-field. But it felt different. When I sit before a game, I am somewhat removed from the thousands of fans standing. But here, I had the intense experience of sitting for the anthem with a sea of people all around. The fight was entertaining, and afterward, I was hanging out at Drai's casino, right next to the Bellagio, in the heart of the strip. I was in the lobby, just taking in the scene. Vegas is one of the great people-watching places on earth.

Suddenly there was a commotion, and I heard someone shout, "Gunshots! Gun! Gun! Shots fired!" There was a stampede to the door, and a bunch of statues were knocked over, the noise adding to the chaos. Then the police stormed in and yelled for people to evacuate the building. You didn't have to tell me twice, and I ran. I wasn't going to go out like that. Like the Batman comics say, "This would be a bad death."

As I was scrambling to safety, police pursued me and forced me to the ground. They cuffed me, as I lay on my stomach, and put a weapon to the back of my head. An officer said if I moved he would "blow [my] f---ing head off." At the same time another officer jammed his knee in my back and cinched the handcuffs on me so tightly my fingers went numb. The knee in my back made me want to squirm involuntarily, but I was scared that if I moved, that could be the only excuse needed to send me to the next life.

With one of those officers on top of me, I couldn't breathe. In great pain, and with a police officer's weapon pointed at my head, all I could think was, *I'm going die for no other reason than I am Black and my skin color is somehow a threat.* I thought about people like Oscar Grant, on his stomach in Fruitvale Station, handcuffed, police gun to the back of his head, and then the trigger was pulled. I thought about Charleena Lyles, how what happened to her could be my fate, and just how unreal it was that only weeks after I'd stood and marched with her family, maybe her family would have to march with mine. I thought about the Seahawks, playing the season with a number 72 patch on their jerseys. But most of all, I thought about whether I would ever kiss my wife again. I thought about whether I would ever see my daughters again, and sit on the floor and play with them. I kept asking, "Sir, what did I do?" and they told me nothing but "Shut the f--- up." There was chaos around me, as the police dragged me across the pavement to the squad car, but I had never felt so alone, so powerless, as my hands and stomach were cut up by the pavement. The arresting officer turned off his body camera before he did this, for reasons that have yet to be explained to me.

Two more officers pushed me into the car. One jerked my head down so hard it wrenched my neck, and another officer slammed me in the stomach and shut the door. I asked over and over what they were charging me with and informed them I had rights that they needed to respect. No one answered me as I sat in the back of that police car.

I suddenly knew what so many Black people before me had experienced: Eric Garner, Michael Brown, Trayvon Martin, Tamir Rice, Charleena Lyles, and too many others to name. I now know what it's like to be treated like an animal. To be a target because of your race. I was guilty until proven innocent, and I knew that this brutality would be justified. After I'd sat in the police car for a period of time, the officers, at my insistence, Googled my name and saw that I was in fact a famous football player (clearly not famous enough), and they let me go. What if I weren't famous? How would my night have ended? It showed me that because equality doesn't live in this country, no matter how much money you make, what job title you have, or how much you give, when you are seen as a "n---a," you will be treated that way.

Afterward, I went public with what happened. I waited a week because I needed to psychologically recover; also, Hurricane Harvey was wrecking Houston, and I didn't want to take focus away from raising funds to help my hometown. When I did go public, the Las Vegas police union accused me of lying. They called on the NFL to investigate my "false statements" and said that my politics around the anthem actions somehow justified this move. They wrote to Roger Goodell, "While the NFL may condone Bennett's disrespect for the American Flag and everything it symbolizes, we hope the league will not ignore Bennett's false accusations against our police officers." The craziest part is that video had already come out that showed exactly what I said had happened: me, on my stomach, hands cuffed, a weapon placed against the back of my head. No charges were brought against me.

And yet, to the police and people who hated that I was speaking out, I'm a liar. Why? Because the officers were Latino, and therefore their actions couldn't have been racial profiling. I don't believe anyone is so stupid as to think being a Black or brown police officer magically prevents you from racial profiling. They also said I was a liar because the LVPD released video of my shaking the officer's hand after being released. Trust me: if you ever feel like your life is in someone else's hands and they let you go, a flood of relief would flow from you as well. I think their real reason for calling me a liar is that their whole worldview is built around the idea that racism in policing doesn't exist. They would rather live in the comfort of that fiction than be forced to confront the uncomfortable truth: that racial profiling is a reality. For some, calling me a liar is also a cover for what they truly think: that I deserved to be abused, and that Black lives simply do not matter.

My belief in this movement is why it was important to me to talk openly, in dueling press conferences with my brother Richard Sherman, about why I support Black Lives Matter. There are so many dishonest ways that this movement is attacked, and Richard gave into the most commonly repeated slander. It's an attack tactic used by some of the same people who have treated Richard like he's the devil with braids: the idea that we don't care about what is called "Black-on-Black crime."

Our back-and-forth started when Richard was falsely accused of "liking" a post online that mentioned killing police. It was all a lie, and Richard held a press conference where he spoke about his support for law enforcement. He then said, "I dealt with a best friend getting killed . . . it was two thirty-five-year-old Black men. Wasn't no police officer involved, wasn't anybody else involved, and I didn't hear anybody shouting 'Black lives matter' then. . . . As long as we have

Black-on-Black crime and one Black man killing another . . . if Black lives matter, then it should matter all the time."

I respected that he was speaking from the heart and felt for his loss. But I also disagreed with his position, and at my own press conference I said, "When people talk about the Black lives matter thing, I think he's misinterpreting it. Yes, Black people kill Black people. White people also kill white people. People kill people every day. This is about social injustice: the people that are supposed to protect them."

I didn't call a press conference because of Richard. We could have talked privately, like we do all the time. He's sharp, and I know he'd listen. I went public because I wanted not just Richard but everyone to realize that looking only at street crime, tragic as it is, ignores the larger problem. The problem is a system that inflicts inadequate schools, lack of clean water, and lack of jobs on the Black community, and police violence is a part of compelling us to accept second-class citizenship. For us, it's a situation of "You were put here to protect us, but who protects us from you?" in too many cities. Police should be a resource for comfort and safety, not a symbol of fear. The point is not that Black lives matter more but that they need to matter as much as everyone else's. Unfortunately, it doesn't look like this society, from the White House down, agrees. I support the Black Lives Matter movement, and I feel it is important for us to stand up and say that until there is true equality, we will not accept the way you are treating us.

Richard and I disagreed. But we also talked about it behind the scenes. I said to him that it's cool for us to see things differently, but, while I respect him and his opinion, I felt I needed to give my perspective so that a different side was presented to the world. I told him I thought there was a larger problem we needed to confront. Yes, I do believe that Black people killing Black people is a major problem. But when people are being killed by those who are supposed to protect them, we need to raise our voices. I also wanted him to understand that the Black Lives Matter movement doesn't involve just Black people. There are white, Latinx, Muslim, Jewish, and Asian supporters in this movement—all types of people who are looking reality in the face and saying that Black lives must matter, also.

I asked Richard to think about everything he has accomplished in this life, and my dude has done a lot. He gives back to the community in ways that get no publicity but directly impact people's lives. He does amazing things. But I asked him to think about why his path has been so hard, and whether it really had to be that way. Behind the scenes, it wasn't just a conversation between Richard and me. It blew up throughout the locker room. There were about ten of us talking, but everyone knew it was going down and pricked up their ears. The discussion was heated but respectful. Everybody had differing opinions, but at the core was an acknowledgment that, as Black professional athletes, we are all exceptions. We have been able to overcome the larger obstacles that most people from our backgrounds would never, ever have had the chance to overcome, simply because we played sports freakishly well. We got pushed through the system in a lot of ways that most people wouldn't, because we are in the athletic top .01 percent.

That is a blessing, but it also comes with a responsibility not to forget those left behind.

We all grew up with so many others who were smarter, more creative, or more analytical than we were, but because their abilities and intelligences were not reflected in sports, they didn't have our opportunities. We have to acknowledge that. We can't be the kind of people who look down on where we came from, with the attitude, "We made it, you should've made it, too." That sends the message that if you can't sing great, rap great, or dance great, if you can't dunk the basketball or run forty yards in under 4.4 seconds, then your ways to get ahead don't exist. That is sick.

I said to Richard, "Bro, look at the system. We can take you to different neighborhoods, whether it's in Ferguson or Houston or Baltimore, and all you have to do is look at schools to know that Black lives do not matter." I told him about my mom, who was a schoolteacher for more than twenty years. She came home from work every day pulling her hair out by the roots, because she knew there was a system keeping people down, and trying to work within that system can feel like shoveling sand in the ocean. We went back and forth. I said that we have to look beyond the issue of "Black-on-Black" crime because segregation dramatically distorts those statistics. If I lived in an all-white neighborhood, the murderers would be white murderers. If I lived in an all-Mexican neighborhood, there would be Mexican-on-Mexican murder. These killings also track entirely by income. Michelle Alexander, the professor who wrote *The New Jim Crow*, published a study on the topic.

Middle-class Black kids are not killing each other, because they're thinking about their college applications.

It was a good discussion, in many ways a great discussion, because we had it publicly and then continued it in the locker room. We used our platform and also were able to expand the consciousness of our brotherhood. Both of those things matter. As for Richard, he was a leading voice in the 2017 off-season, speaking out for Kaepernick and speaking out for me after my experience in Las Vegas with the reality of racial profiling that we face.

My evolution toward supporting the Black Lives Matter movement and sitting for the anthem can also come down to three names: Trayvon, Ferguson, and Kaepernick. When Trayvon Martin was killed in Sanford, Florida, I was living with my family about a hundred miles away because I was playing in Tampa Bay. I remember hearing the news and being instantly stunned, knowing this would go national. He was seventeen years old, hunted down and killed for going out at halftime of the NBA All-Star Game to buy some iced tea and Skittles, and they wouldn't even arrest his killer. I just sat back and thought: *This young boy didn't even get to experience the world. He didn't really get to live or have his own family or know what it feels like to kiss your wife and tell her you'll be back for dinner, or see his kids graduate from college. He'll never be able to show his mom her new grandkids. That experience was taken.*

It hit me and many across the country so hard. The white people who weren't on right-wing talk radio trying to somehow make excuses for his death, as if wearing a hoodie should be a death sentence, were shocked, saying, "This still happens?" But Black people were saying, "Again? Another kid?" If any other race were losing kids the way Black families are losing kids, it would be a national emergency. If a white kid had been shot by some stalker pretending to be a police officer, and the shooter at first wasn't even arrested and then was set free, everybody would have lost their minds. But too many people didn't care. They didn't care that the killer—and I don't say his name—was a vigilante, not a police officer. They didn't care that he hunted down this young man even after a 911 dispatcher told him to stop. After Trayvon was brought to the morgue, they drug-tested him but not his killer. People didn't care.

Then came the 2014 killing of Michael Brown by officer Darren Wilson in Ferguson, Missouri, which happened when I was back in Seattle. This was the first "social media death," where the mourning was made all the more raw because Michael Brown's body was left lying in the street for hours, and we all saw it live-streamed: the people crying, horrified that he was being treated worse than garbage. I remember seeing this and just thinking, *Do I even want a Black son?* That was going through my head. It breaks my heart to share that.

Then people fought back, made history, and launched this movement. When the Ferguson rebellion popped off, our locker room came together to talk about it as a team. We had to talk about it because footage of the fires and teargas and police in a tank was on TV in the training room. It was everywhere. There were ten small discussions happening around different lockers, and as a leader, you have to know when to bring people together. Several of us were telling others on our team that Ferguson was familiar territory, that this was not new. There may be new technology, new phones, new ways to zap these images around the world in a heartbeat, and new military hardware being used by police. But it's the same murders. It's the same kids being targeted. It's little different than in the 1960s. Heck, the classrooms in Ferguson probably still used textbooks from the 1960s. Some of us were shocked that this had happened in America. Others of us were jaded. But what we all had in common was trying to grasp why this was still happening in the twenty-first century, and how the country could see us as heroes on the field and as disposable off the field.

We played St. Louis just two weeks later, and the players on the Rams came out on the field with the "Hands up, don't shoot" pose. When I saw them with their hands up, I was all for it. Those who did it were all offensive players, like wide receiver Kenny Britt and running back Tre Mason. I was so proud of them it almost made me sad that I was going to have to knock the snot out of them. I supported the Rams' action, especially because Ferguson is a forgotten part of their city, and as they were bringing Michael Brown's death to *Monday Night Football*, a military crackdown was happening just a few miles away. It takes that kind of solidarity to make any kind of change.

When we played the 49ers soon after, I got a sack and struck the same pose, "Hands up, don't shoot." A lot of white people still don't understand what that slogan even means. They counter with the disputed argument that Michael

Brown's hands weren't up, therefore the very gesture spreads a lie about how he was killed. That's not the issue. "Hands up, don't shoot" speaks to the fact that you can do everything right when interacting with the police. You can hold your hands up high, remember every detail of "the talk" with your parents, and still be shot. Ask Terence Crutcher of Tulsa, Oklahoma. His murder was all caught on video: he walked toward officer Betty Shelby, his hands held up high, and he was still struck down. Even though this was videotaped, she wasn't only let free. She got her job back, along with back pay, and the killing will be wiped from her employment record. She literally is getting away with murder.

As I've said, people call the NFL the "No Fun League." They will fine you if you've got the wrong color shoelaces on. Yet, after Ferguson, when players were raising their hands and writing things like "My children's lives matter" on their uniforms, the league office didn't come down with fines. (I tried to do something a little more fresh and wear cleats with Muhammad Ali and Malcolm X airbrushed on, but they said I couldn't. Too bad; I liked those cleats.) The bigger point is that I think Roger Goodell is still a human being, so maybe he felt something. Even though some might think he's an owner-controlled hand puppet, he had a human response to that moment back in 2014. Not to say that NFL headquarters supports the movement, but at that particular moment they could tell it wasn't the best time to crush players who spoke out or altered their uniforms a fraction. Also, Black men make up 70 percent of the players. I think they knew if they tried to crack down on us, they'd open up a major battle. Maybe the pain of

Trayvon Martin's family, the pain of Mike Brown's family, and the pain of the entire town of Ferguson was enough for them to say, "Let the players express what they are feeling."

Of course, the limits of what they're willing to accept were exposed when Colin Kaepernick took the Black Lives Matter protest to the national anthem. Colin opened up so many eyes and took so much abuse for stepping out first. It hurt him that he is a quarterback, the face of a franchise. He was also at the end of his contract. The courage to do what he did, given his situation, is greatly undervalued. As I said earlier, I'm sitting during the anthem in part because I'm not going to let the memory of Colin's action die, and I know I'm not alone. NFL executives have talked anonymously to the media about Kaepernick, and it's a sin, the things they've said, without giving their names. They've compared him to Rae Carruth, a Carolina Panthers wide receiver who had his pregnant girlfriend killed. He had her killed! And that's how they've categorized Colin. They are scared of Black men who overcome the fear to stand up. So many people can't handle that. That's why the lives of powerful Black men and women have been destroyed or simply snatched. Who would want to step up, given those risks? But still we do.

When I read a biography of Fred Hampton, it was clear that he was aware of the risks to his personal safety, but he also knew he had the power to change lives. He knew he could make Black lives matter. Then there is my hero Muhammad Ali. The public only embraced him after he lost the power of speech, late in his life. But Muhammad Ali, to me, was always a hero, because he talked all kinds of smack about politics,

Nixon, and Black life, and he backed it up. He was willing to say what needed to be said, no matter the persecution. He lived by a code that is easy to say but so hard to follow: speak the truth, even if it hurts. And if you don't agree with something, don't mumble around it.

When he was explaining why he refused to fight in Vietnam, Ali said it and made it plain: "I don't agree with killing the Viet Cong. They didn't do anything to me. They never called me n----r! People here call me n----r every day. You won't let me in the restaurant. My wife can't even go to the same store. And you're telling me I should go to the white man's war?" My commitment to Black Lives Matter is to make sure that people like Fred Hampton and Muhammad Ali did not die in vain. We will build on what they brought to our lives. It's called standing on the shoulders of giants.

My open commitment to the Black Lives Matter movement, beyond on-field gestures, social media posts, and locker room debates, started in Seattle at an event in 2016 called Black Lives Matter in Schools. Teachers planning to teach Black history at a local elementary school had received death threats. When that kind of thing happens in your community, you have to step up. For the day of the event, the Seattle teachers union asked all the educators in the city to wear Black Lives Matter shirts in protest, and it was a huge success. More than three thousand out of the five thousand total Seattle teachers, of all races and ethnicities, wore the shirts to school. Then they held a rally, and I was a part of it. Being there made me feel like people must have felt in the 1960s when they first heard about

Black Power, except this was more multiracial and united across color, which made it all the more moving to me. I felt a wave of love for being Black and love for looking the way I do: love of my skin, love of my shade, love for the way my hair grows out. I already loved my beard, so I was good there.

I went up on stage, and teachers and students started asking me questions, thanking me for being there but also challenging me to think about what I was doing and whether I could do more. It was a life-changing moment for me, and I just laid it all out, pledging my support and explaining what some of the Seahawks players could do to support the efforts of this amazing community. I figured that no matter what I said, somebody was going to find something wrong with it. So I might as well be authentic and honest.

People thought Black Lives Matter was a fad or that it was going to die out. But I hope we realize that this goes way beyond just a hashtag. To me, this movement is not only about responding to police violence. Not at all. I see Black and brown people losing their lives. I see white people dying of opioid overdoses. It seems like people don't want to live anymore. People don't want to be in a world where they feel they're not valued. They're checking out early. They're thinking, "Why live through this?" We need to give each other hope. Imagine you are walking down the street and see someone getting beaten in a shadowy corner. You immediately ask yourself, *Should I help, or do I mind my own business? Do I choose silence or do I take action?* That's how I view everything. Society says that you shouldn't get involved because it's not your problem, but your conscience tells you that you should speak up because you know, deep down inside, that this is the right thing to do. That's the battle we have with ourselves every day. Most people lose that battle because they think, "I don't want to risk looking stupid or getting hurt or wasting my time. Better to just send a tweet." But we need to do more than that, and we need to reach out beyond where it's comfortable.

When Black people talk about Black people's problems, the problems never get solved. I want to push white people to think about their roles, to think about how these issues affect them also, to think about how when we come together we can confront common ills that exist in all communities, Black, brown, and white, that have been left behind. We could come together or we could blame each other. But we're not going to come together without trust, and I don't see trust being built until white people say, "Black lives need to matter as much as white ones."

When a white person gets involved, other people take notice—the people whose kids aren't being killed in the streets. That's when we will see change. This is something for all of us to organize around, wherever we stand. Where I stand happens to be in the National Football League. And when white players step up and speak out, it changes the whole dynamic. It's been so gratifying to see white players begin to move in that direction. When Justin Britt, Chris Long, and Seth De-Valve got involved in the anthem actions, it brought an entire white audience into the dialogue and shifted the conversation, even if only a little bit. That solidarity, as it grows, can change the world.

INTER-SECTIONALITY ALSO MATTERS

You're not designed to thrive by yourself.

—**Maya Moore**

Solidarity is the idea that we can organize around a common goal—uniting across our differences in skin color or gender or sexuality—to make a better world for future generations. It's why I stood with the Palestinian people. It's why I stood with the Women's Strike for Equality, and it's why I wore a Bernie Sanders hat around NFL locker rooms. But we will get to all that.

Intersectionality is related, but different. It's a big word but means something very simple. It's the understanding that an individual can experience multiple types of injustice and that although our struggles may be different, they overlap or intersect. Intersectionality clicked for me when I thought about Charleena Lyles. She was killed because of racism, no doubt, but her life as a Black woman—not just as a Black person—is critical to understanding her death. Charleena had suffered sexual assault and violence, and she called the police in the first place because she was worried that an abusive former lover was coming back to hurt her. I understand what it's like to be Black and feel like your life is in the hands of a police officer pointing a weapon at you. But combining that with the fear of violence because you're a woman is something I had never experienced. I realized that I needed to understand the impact of both the racism and the sexism in not only her death but also how the incident played out afterward, when she was painted as an unfit mother—as if that justified killing her in front of her children. This understanding of how multiple oppressions can overlap is the meaning of intersectionality.

Years before I knew what intersectionality was, before I even knew the word existed, I felt it when I learned how Muhammad Ali connected the struggle of Black people in this country with the devastation of the Vietnamese people and his push to end the US war in Vietnam. If you have never read his words before, if you only know Muhammad Ali as a poster, a T-shirt, or the dude played in the movie by Will Smith, read this speech he gave at a fair-housing rally in his hometown of Louisville, Kentucky, back in 1968:

> Why should they ask me to put on a uniform and go ten thousand miles from home and drop bombs and bullets on brown people in Vietnam while so-called Negro people in

Louisville are treated like dogs and denied simple human rights? No, I'm not going ten thousand miles from home to help murder and burn another poor nation simply to continue the domination of white slave masters of the darker people the world over. This is the day when such evils must come to an end. I have been warned that to take such a stand would cost me millions of dollars. But I have said it once and I will say it again: the real enemy of my people is here. I will not disgrace my religion, my people, or myself by becoming a tool to enslave those who are fighting for their own justice, freedom, and equality. . . . If I thought the war was going to bring freedom and equality to twenty-two million of my people, they wouldn't have to draft me, I'd join tomorrow. I have nothing to lose by standing up for my beliefs. So I'll go to jail, so what? We've been in jail for four hundred years.

That's intersectionality to me. Muhammad Ali wasn't Vietnamese. He had never been to Saigon. He—like most Americans at the time—probably couldn't have found Vietnam on a map. But he identified with what they were going through: their pain sounded like his pain. They shared the common experience of being brutalized by those in power, though Ali noted their realities were very different: he wasn't being bombed. Ali offered solidarity, hope, and even his own freedom in support of their struggle.

The Olympic protestors Tommie Smith and John Carlos also taught me about intersectionality. Nobody remembers who won all the medals at the 1968 Mexico City Olympics, but every time I see that photo of their fists in the air on the medal stand, I'm reminded that it wasn't just a Black project but a human rights project. When you dig deeper into the history, you learn that they weren't just standing up for themselves. They were standing with the people of South Africa and Rhodesia, who were living under a racist system called apartheid. You learn that the all-white Harvard crew team stood with them and even created the buttons they wore on the medal stand, which read, "Olympic Project for Human Rights."

The Black Panther Fred Hampton also taught me about intersectionality. Everyone should know more about Fred Hampton. He was killed—executed—by the Chicago police, teamed up with the FBI, when he was just twenty-one years old, and his loss continues to be felt. Hampton was so far ahead of his time that we're still catching up. He saw working with Native Americans, poor white people, and gay people as essential to the Black struggle. He created the first "rainbow coalition"—it was logical to him to find connections between different struggles, but somewhere along the way, since his death, we've lost that logic. Today, we are fighting for Black Lives Matter and Black liberation, but we will succeed only if we can figure out how to connect our struggle with every other effort out there for justice and equality. That's why you see me working with Native Americans, Palestinians, women, and people in Africa and Haiti.

To practice intersectionality, I believe you have to remove yourself from the fear or discomfort of associating with certain groups or issues you've been taught to ignore. I know Black people who don't care about immigrants, men who don't care about women, and straight people who don't care about gay people. Why are we like this? Why don't we care? Maybe we are so divided by tribe that we're taught that caring for someone outside our assigned category is the ultimate sin, yet I would argue that it's the ultimate expression of being part of the human family. You grow and come to understand that there's so much more to this world than just your bubble. You learn that we can't organize along the same lines that keep us divided.

Intersectionality has to be a part of our thinking if we are ever going to see change. We need to take to heart Dr. King's words that injustice anywhere is a threat to justice everywhere. Right now, being an immigrant—or even looking like you might be an immigrant from what some people call "s---hole countries"—means having a target on your back. Muslims, refugees, and Latinxs, in particular, are living through terror. Anti-Latinx hate crimes have increased by 50 percent in the last five years, with a big spike since the start of Trump's presidential campaign, when he called Mexican immigrants "rapists." The school-to-prison pipeline divides us as well, with Latinx youth three times more likely to be suspended, expelled, or referred to court than white students who do the same things. You are three times more likely to live behind bars if you are Latinx than if you are white. Then there is the issue of wealth: the average Latinx household has only 8 percent of the wealth of the average white household, and they make 67 cents for every dollar a white man earns. A Latinx has to work 22 months to earn what white workers of similar educational levels make in a year. Until we confront these realities, how can we possibly tell people that education and hard work alone are enough to make the change we are so desperate to see? Intersectionality as a political approach allows us to make these connections and unite.

As for being Muslim? Wow. The number of assaults against Muslims in the United States rose like crazy between 2015 and 2016. According to the Pew Research Center, it's worse now than it was after 9/11. That means assaults, vandalism, and broken windows. Those people who march with the tiki torches think they're tough. But they're afraid. They are afraid to face what the United States has done to other countries around the world, resulting in thousands upon thousands of people seeking to come here. They are afraid of confronting their own bigotry. They are afraid of losing power.

There are people who might give me a break if I only talked about Black Lives Matter, because I'm Black. But when I start talking about rights for other people, I'm marked. I think we get attacked for standing up for others precisely because doing so opens an avenue for change, and change threatens the status quo and those in positions of power. And that can bring you all kinds of unwanted attention. Unwanted attention that's a little bit more serious than jumping offsides in the fourth quarter or being on TMZ.

Intersectionality depends on collaboration. Collaboration is how a message has the potential to catch on like wildfire. You can't build the Statue of Liberty by yourself. You need teams of people who want to build it with you. You need sisters and brothers willing to carry the bricks and the cement. You need everyone to offer up their special skills. You have to ask, "Do we all believe in this goal? If so, then who knows how to design? Who knows how to hammer? Who knows how to spread the word?" This goes back to Fred Hampton, who said that the goal of any movement is to help people believe in themselves and understand that they have the potential to remake the world. Most people don't see that in themselves.

Intersectionality is why I made a decision to turn down a trip to visit Israel. I wanted to go, but not if it meant seeing only one side. It wasn't easy for me, because I knew how bad the backlash would be. I knew that when I made this decision some people were going to say, "That guy is the enemy. I don't want to cheer for him no more. I don't want to buy his jersey no more. He is dead to us." That was a given. But I also didn't know if someone might go as far as saying, "I want to kill his family. I want to do whatever is needed to keep him from talking again." But my reasons for turning down this trip and doing so as publicly as possible were in step with my morals and my beliefs. I want to take the opportunity to explain, because it's a perfect example of how the intersectional approach works in my mind.

Eleven NFL players were slated to be part of a "goodwill" delegation to Israel, all expenses paid. When I was asked to do it, my first thought was, "Hey! Free trip to Israel. First-class tickets! Why not?" I didn't really do any background research on what the trip was, where I would be allowed to go, and who I would be able to talk to, so I can honestly say that was my fault, and I will never make that mistake again. A few weeks before we were set to leave, the *Times of Israel* ran an article about the trip that described it as a highly organized, Israeli government–designed operation with the aim of turning me and the other NFL players into "goodwill ambassadors," who would return to the United States to "fight perceptions" of the country. I learned that the trip would pretty much isolate us from the Palestinian people. I had to ask why they intentionally did not want to expose us to the entire country. I had visited other countries all over the world, and none had ever asked me to be a "goodwill ambassador." To truly be a goodwill ambassador, you need to see both sides so you can represent what is happening.

It made me concerned about the entire trip, but before I decided not to go, I knew I had to educate myself on the situation over there. I had to be humble enough to realize that I knew very little about Israel and Palestine, so I went on a crash course about the history of the region. It was like cramming for a final exam. I locked myself in my room. I spoke to scholars and academics. I picked up a stack of books from every angle so I could do my own research. The life-altering point was reading a book called *Freedom Is a Constant Struggle*, written by Angela Davis in 2015. I learned that Black Lives Matter activists had created all kinds of bonds and communications with the Palestinian people, and that there was a mural of Michael Brown on the Palestinian side of the separation wall that Israel built around a place called Gaza, where more than a million Palestinians live behind that wall. They were even communicating over Skype about how best to deal with teargas: instead of using water to flush your eyes, use milk. I can honestly say that, as a man, I cried when I read about this connection. In such a dark time in our country, I felt inspired.

Pele asked me, "Why are you so emotional about this?" And I told her I hadn't known how bad it was, and the strength of people in impossible situations had touched my soul.

That's when I knew I had to step up and not only refuse the trip but also tell the truth about why I wasn't going. I think it bothered some people that I didn't go, but I'd seen some things in my reading and research that I couldn't unsee. I'd seen, in my mind's eye, the kids, the women, the men, the checkpoints, the schools, the sewage in the streets, the poverty, and the wall. I felt a kinship with a struggle that in so many ways reminds me of the civil rights movement or the anti-apartheid movement in South Africa. I realized that I wouldn't be the person I aspire to be if I called out injustice here at home and just stopped at our border. It doesn't work that way.

One of the most powerful moments in this journey was when I received a call from this legend, Angela Davis—not only is she a hero of mine, but I had just read her book. This was the first time we had ever spoken, and since then we've become friends, which is trippy. Angela Davis took the time to share with me her personal experiences of traveling through Palestine and seeing how the Palestinians were treated, their living conditions, the history of how their land was taken away from them by illegal settlements, and how they are all collectively punished for the violent actions of a few. I also spoke to Palestinian American scholar and professor Noura Erakat and ended up meeting with her students at Georgetown, including Israeli students. In talking to Angela Davis and Noura Erakat, I realized I had empathy and identification with the Palestinian people that I didn't know existed inside of me. We're dealing with police violence here, and what they are dealing with there sounds too familiar to ignore. After educating myself on the subject, I felt that the only moral thing for me to do was to stand on the right side of history, to stand on the shoulders of my ancestors and be a bridge between oppressed people. Palestine was no different. I might not have thought too much about their situation before this, but now it just wasn't acceptable, and I wasn't going to be used in that way.

The next decision was whether to quietly refuse to go and make up an excuse, or to share my thoughts with the world. I chose the latter and wrote the following open letter:

Dear World,

I was scheduled to make a visit to Israel with fellow NFL players. I was excited to see this remarkable and historic part of the world with my own eyes. I was not aware, until reading this article about the trip in the *Times of Israel*, that my itinerary was being constructed by the Israeli government for the purposes of making me, in the words of a government official, an "influencer and opinion-former," who would then be "an ambassador of good will." I will not be used in such a manner. When I do go to Israel—and I do plan to go—it will be to see not only Israel but also the West Bank and Gaza so I can see how the Palestinians, who have called this land home for thousands of years, live their lives.

One of my heroes has always been Muhammad Ali. I know that Ali always stood strongly with the Palestinian people, visiting refugee camps, going to rallies, and always willing to be a "voice for the voiceless." I want to be a "voice for the voiceless," and I cannot do that by going on this kind of trip to Israel.

I know that this will anger some people and inspire others. But please know that I did this not for you, but to be in accord with my own values and my own conscience. Like 1968 Olympian John Carlos always says, "There is no partial commitment to justice. You are either in or you're out." Well, I'm in.

Sincerely,

Michael Bennett

When I posted the letter to my Instagram account, I had no idea that it would become front-page news in Israel and a topic of debate throughout Europe. It was crazy. They don't even like American football in Europe, but they were talking about me. Sometimes you just throw a stone out there and hope for a ripple, and sometimes the stone starts a tidal wave.

It was a big deal. The response was political whiplash, a storm of attention about a situation where I was just learning the basics. As pro athletes, we're stuck in a world where our days start at 6:00 a.m., we don't get done until 6:00 p.m., and when we get home, we play with the kids, eat dinner, get our rest, and then do it all over again. The world around us is like a rumor, a barely noticeable buzz that needs to roar if we are going to pay it any attention. What was so cool about this experience was that the buzz did become a roar, and minds were opened to both critical thinking and the effect athletes can have on the world. By the time you're reading this book, I will be making plans to travel to Israel and Palestine on a trip not designed by the government, so I can explore everything about that part of the world—the good, the bad, and the ugly—for myself.

In addition to learning about the politics and history, the best part of this experience is that now the last thing many people want to talk about with me is football. I love that, because if people only know you for what you do on the field, obviously they're only going to talk to you about sports. When people know more about what you believe in, what your morals are, you'll have better conversations. People want to hear more, and I am willing to say more. It's beautiful. People asking me about football all the time gets old. It's like being a plumber and all people want to talk to you about is toilets. If I were a plumber, I might still have my passion for toilets, but I'd also need a break when the plunger goes back in the closet.

This desire to link people up and push forward for united change is also why I supported senator Bernie Sanders for president in 2016. I wore a Bernie Sanders baseball hat both to press conferences and in the locker room. Heck, I wore that Bernie Sanders hat all around Seattle. I liked what he was talking about, so one day I snatched the hat from the head of a friend. I was like, "Man, give me that Bernie Sanders hat!" He said, "You want this hat, for real?" I said, "I'll wear that hat every day!" I did, and in Seattle people went crazy for it. People love Bernie in Seattle like they love coffee. But outside the Seattle zone, people were talking like this was the weirdest thing they had ever seen: a football player supporting Bernie Sanders. It didn't compute for them. The dude won twenty-three states in the Democratic primary and had the most support among people under thirty of anyone running, so, to me, it was a great fit. People would ask me, in surprise, "Are you some kind of a socialist?" And I would answer, "I just love the idea of everybody having opportunity." I got the "Be careful who you associate with!" line, but I was associating less with the man than with the idea—for example—that the government, instead of spending my tax money on prisons, should invest in communities that have been starved for too long.

All the stuff Bernie was talking about was so real to me because those are the issues, the real issues that human beings are dealing with and talking about at home. He wasn't talking about building a wall or saying America has always been great. He was putting forward big ideas about wiping out student debt and giving young people the opportunity to grow. He reminded me of my mom, asking big questions, like, "Why shouldn't there be free higher education? It costs hundreds of thousands of dollars if you want to be a doctor. How many people want to be doctors but can't?" That's the kind of questioning I think is so vital to our future. But because I agreed with a lot of the stuff Bernie was saying, people were mad at me. I didn't care. I'm free to like what he was about: how he approached the world, his ideals, and the fact that he was even raising these questions. A lot of people said his ideas were too far-fetched and could never happen, but hey, Donald Trump happened. I don't want to hear about anything being "far-fetched" ever again.

Bernie Sanders actually called my parents' house in Houston, looking to connect, and my dad forgot to tell me. My phone number is not listed, but Bernie's people saw me on television wearing his hat and knew I was from Houston, so they tracked down my dad's number and called to see if I could go to a rally in Texas. I was so mad at my dad. Weeks later, he said, "Oh, by the way, I forgot to tell you. Bernie Sanders called."

I was like, "Dad! Bernie Sanders called the house and wanted to talk to me?! I would've flown to Texas for that!" I cooled off, but man, for a second I was mad at my dad like I was a salty teenager.

But as much as I was into Bernie, I also believe that just electing someone and expecting them to make real change happen for us is a dead end. I believe in intersectionality because Bernie Sanders—or anyone else—isn't going to end racism or bring resources into underserved communities. We are going to need to connect with each other to bring about these shifts. I hope we have more political candidates who express the values Bernie was talking about, but we still have to do the work.

My parents raised me to challenge the system and to question facts when they are presented to me. You have to question the way things are, because curiosity is what drives the future. Questions are the starting point for making any kind of change. This is how I approach the world, and this is how we are raising our daughters, so their future can be whatever they want it to be.

OUR DAUGHTERS AND THE POWER OF WOMEN

My message is to never quit, never give up. When you have a little trouble here and there, just keep fighting. In the end, it will pay off.

—**Gabby Douglas**

When I decided not to stand for the anthem, I did one interview where I said, "I love hot dogs like any other American. I love football like any other American. But I don't love segregation, I don't love riots, I don't love oppression. I don't love gender slander."

That statement made a lot of people do a double take. Not the part about loving hot dogs. I do love hot dogs as long as they're all beef and aren't the kind with the rat droppings. That's nasty. It was the part about "gender slander."

197

That is very important to me, and I make sure that supporting women's rights and speaking out against sexism are central to everything I do. Some of that comes from the strong women I've always had in my life: my mother, my grandmothers, my aunties, and on down the line. "Strong minded" doesn't begin to describe the women in the Bennett family. One of my grandmas, Rebecca, is where I get my attitude. She's a spunky old woman with a bad attitude, but at the same time she's the most loving person in the world. That's what makes her so special and so crazy: she'll cut you down and then be the first person crying when you leave.

But I can say that the push to link any work I do to the struggle for women's rights starts with the woman I met when she was fifteen and I was sixteen, who has become more than a wife, more than a partner: an intertwined spirit. We've now been together more than half our lives, and it's the deepest possible connection I can imagine having with another human being. The greatest gift we've given each other over the years is seeing each other evolve from the kids we were in high school to the people we are today. Think about how much you change from age fifteen to thirty. There were no guarantees we would grow in the same way. Teenage relationships don't usually last for that reason. But here we are today, making this journey together, shoulder to shoulder.

Pele stands beside me, not behind me. I could never be serious about changing the world if I lacked the belief that my wife can be a community leader, a philanthropist, an activist, and a changemaker. I owe her so much because, to be truthful, it is only through her eyes that I have come to see the problems of the world. I would be blind to the people's pain without her. Her empathy is like an electrical current that runs between us and flows from her mind to mine. I am at the point where I would die for what I believe in, and I can say honestly that I would never have come this far without meeting Pele and loving her to the point that I would lay down my life for her. From being a teenage mother, when we had nothing but un- certainty, to the present moment, when she is using the power of her voice and her convictions to affect people, I sometimes look at her and shake my head, amazed by the person she is still becoming. Her love has taught me to love.

For both of us, this journey would have been impossible without the ultimate changemakers in our own lives, our three daughters: Peyton, Blake, and Ollie. Having daughters has allowed me to be kind, to be unafraid, and to be emotional. They've cured me of thinking about myself first. It's the best thing that has ever happened to me. I've had people try to discredit me as a man by saying, "Well, you don't have a son." I laugh in their faces and say, "Who cares? My daughters will be better than any man I could ever create. They're the future." I look at my family completely differently from people who have an obsession with the gender of a child. I think, "I have three young, curious people in my life, and they can be who- ever they want to be."

If I had a son, he would carry the burden of having ev- eryone in his life ask him if he was going to follow in my shoes and play in the NFL, and I have some big shoes to fill. For every Clay Matthews or Peyton Manning, whose dads were in the NFL, I can point you to a mess of young people who tried to follow their fathers into this game, only to meet with disappointment and dashed dreams. It would be even harder for my son than, say, Mark Ingram, a running back for the Saints, whose dad played wide receiver back in the day. That's because a son of mine would have to fight me to get onto the field. I felt like I had to play football. Any son of mine would not. He'd be pressured by friends and coaches to play, and he would hear from his mom and me that the safety of his brain and body was too important for all that.

But when it comes to our daughters, we don't have the burden of football on their future or what other people say their ambitions should be. No one puts them in that box. They can be whoever and whatever they want. They can be astronauts or create a cartoon series, like their Uncle Tellus, about being an astronaut. It's all there for them. I have one daughter who wants to cure malaria, another who wants to be a dentist, and another who wants to be a veterinarian. Some days they say they want to be singers or princesses or soccer players. I love the creativity of their minds and the fact that they truly feel they can be whoever they want to be. Pele and I wrote a children's book about our kids called *Three Little Monsters Have a Wild Day*. They can tear it up when things aren't sitting right, but they are also so cute that it's tough to stay mad. My youngest daughter, she can be a monster for sure. Some days I'm like, "Yeah, you could've gotten three sacks today with that attitude!"

I know they're going to be something greater than I am, because the things I have done are primarily around sports.

I'm branching out, but the center of my life at this time has to be football. My daughters really have a chance to change lives. I'm excited about it. Every day I tell my wife, "Oh, I can't wait! Six more years and Peyton is going to college and she's going to be *this*!" Whenever I go on trips, like to Haiti or Japan or South Dakota, my family goes with me. It's not just about my growth. It's about growing together as a family—not just living on screens but staring the reality of the world in the face, because if they don't see the truth of what's out there, the world will never change. That's something I want for every child. When I look in my children's eyes and they are seeing the possibility of being changemakers in this world, it feels like a miracle. When I go to a youth prison and look into the eyes of a child the same age as my oldest daughter, but the light—that spark—is out, it tears me up inside. I do what I can for my daughters, but the truth is that they do something even better for me.

I try to see the world through my daughters' eyes, thinking about what they will have to experience on their journeys as Black women, and it keeps me up nights. The more I imagine what is headed their way, the more determined I am to see change. We can't change anything unless we talk about it. According to the Department of Justice, 40 to 60 percent of Black women report having been sexually assaulted by age eighteen, and a shocking 40 percent of Black women are assaulted by their husbands or partners. When you factor in how much sexual violence goes underreported, this is even more disturbing.

The abuse of Black women goes back to our arrival in this country in chains. Enslaved African women were beaten and raped as if they weren't even human. That made their hurt and pain seem like something normal, and it continues to this day.

This is only a part of what my daughters are going to have to confront. The United States also has one of the highest rates on the planet of women who die during childbirth, a rate that has doubled since 1987. This is a national disgrace, and it is even worse for Black women. According to ProPublica, Black women are three to four times more likely than white women to die while giving birth. Even Serena Williams almost died during childbirth. Serena Williams!

Researchers say that they can't explain these mortality stats. They cite risk factors such as high blood pressure, obesity, and diabetes, but then they tell the world that the cause of increased maternal death for Black women is unknown. That is either ignorance or cowardice in the face of obvious truths. The cause is the weight of racism, sexism, and the stress that Black women have had to carry for generations as the heart of families, while they earn sixty-three cents for every dollar a white man earns. That's the cause. The greatest testament to "Black girl magic" I can think of, other than the daily miracles my girls create, is the way Black women have persevered despite centuries spent trying to bring them down.

Now that I have daughters, I understand further what women's rights are all about. They have become immediate and urgent to me, when they weren't before. This is just me, being honest. Women's issues were someone else's problem, and because I'm a man, I felt like it was not mine. But knowing that sexism and gender violence and employment discrimination are going to be real obstacles in their lives makes me want to fight for girls and women with all my heart. I wish it didn't take having daughters for men to realize that this is their struggle, too. It should be enough that we are all human and we should want equality. But the reality is we live in a world where women—especially Black women—aren't valued, and that often means that until we are looking at the world through our daughters' eyes, we just don't get it like we should.

My daughters are the reason I am working with an organization called iamtheCODE, the first African-led global movement to mobilize government and private sector investors to advance STEAMED (Science, Technology, Engineering, Arts, Mathematics, Entrepreneurship, and Design) education. I got involved because I want to expand opportunities for girls to be whoever they want. This became a focus of mine after a random exchange with an old friend from back home. We were catching up, and I told him I had three daughters, and do you know the first thing he said to me? Not "Congratulations" or even "That's cool!" He said, "Oh, you better get a shotgun. That's going to be hard." Why can't people say, "You have daughters, man they're going to be blessed. They're going to be something great." If I had a son, they would say, "Your son is going to be the greatest player ever!" So I wanted to fund and develop an organization that could encourage girls to pursue the kinds of jobs where they'll be sitting at the table and creating the new world.

Then there's the idea that I need a shotgun to "protect them." That is so absurdly sexist, it's crazy. It denies the ability of a young girl to have aspirations higher than being an Instagram model. It dumbs down my relationship with them to being the guardian of their bodies instead of a champion of their minds and their personal and political growth.

I want to teach my daughters, above all else, that their generation is going to be decisive, and that as young people, they need to get off their behinds and realize the power they have. They are the future. I tell them that if you don't like the type of education you are receiving, you should research something yourself. You can look up anything you want—but please, check the sources. You can teach yourself to do almost anything with YouTube. Right now, I could go look up how to fix a refrigerator and actually find a step-by-step tutorial.

Unlike in past generations, the information is out there. It's a click away. But if you don't have a thirst for it, you'll be on screen all day, watching other people play videogames or "Top 30 Wardrobe Malfunctions." We absolutely need great teachers, but young people can't wait for someone else to educate them. They have to educate themselves. And they have the power to do it.

I am also vigilant about what my daughters are taught in their schools. We live in Hawaii during the off-season, and when I learned that my daughters weren't studying Black history in their classes in Hawaii, I connected with a local historian and we put together a Black History Month program for the school. In the process I learned that Black history is central to Hawaiian history. The first African people arrived in Hawaii by the early 1800s, and Black people held it down on the island for centuries. Now I'm on the board of the Hawaiian Africana Museum, which is an actual thing. I did this for my daughters, but a side benefit is that I'm researching and learning stuff I didn't know and was never taught in school. The other day a senior citizen told me about a subject she was researching. I asked at what point she would be satisfied with everything she knew, and she said, "To be honest, I'm a lifetime learner." That blew my mind because it's the honest truth. There is always something new to learn.

Thinking through an intersectional lens, I supported the Women's March after Trump was elected. Several months later, I put out a written statement in solidarity with the Women's Strike for Equality on International Women's Day, in March 2017:

> As a black man in America, I sometimes get overwhelmed and discouraged by what I see—from the police killings of unarmed black men to the unequal educational system to the mass incarceration of poor people of color in for-profit prisons. But when I look in my daughters' eyes, I see the courage of Harriet Tubman, the patience of Rosa Parks, the soul of Ida B. Wells, the passion of Fannie Lou Hamer, and the heart of Angela Davis. I see the future. I see hope. And I'm inspired because it will be women who lead the future. That is why I am writing to express my unconditional solidarity with the women's strike on International Women's Day, March 8. It would be easy for me to say that I am supporting this day of resistance because I have three daughters and I want nothing to stand in their way as they attempt to achieve their goals. I could also say that I am doing this because my wife, Pele—my best friend and soulmate—is of Samoan descent and has lived the struggle of being a

woman and the daughter of immigrants. But this issue is a lot bigger than my dreams for my own family. It's about the women across the earth who are suffering: women who are less worried about a glass ceiling than they are about a collapsing floor. It's about women of color across the earth who live on less than one dollar a day. It's about all women who are subject to sexual assault and violence. I stand with the women's strike because I agree with the unity statement from the strike's platform, which reads that this day is "organized by and for women who have been marginalized and silenced by decades of neoliberalism directed towards working women, women of color, Native women, disabled women, immigrant women, Muslim women, lesbian, queer and trans women." I encourage my fellow football players to join me in standing with these brave women from across the world. As Angela Davis once said, "To understand how any society functions you must understand the relationship between the men and the women." By that metric, our society is failing. We need change, and to quote Frederick Douglass, "If there is no struggle there is no progress."

Sincerely,

Michael Bennett

I had been doing work on women's issues, but this was my opportunity to make that bridge between philanthropy and activism. I was buzzing with it, doing my best impression of Sojourner Truth, saying, "This is the time for women. A day that men have to stand up and speak the truth for women." I posted this letter online because I wanted women to know there are men out there supporting the women's movement. I can see through my daughters' eyes just how many obstacles girls and women face. Their brains, their achievements, their creativity, and their place in society can be cut down, and it's not like we have tons of smart men making the world a better place. We need all hands on deck.

Not only am I willing to say that I support women—the definition of all talk—but I'm also going to help create more programs for women and girls and collaborate with great women who are already doing amazing things. In New York City I spoke out for a group that provides support for survivors of domestic violence. One of my friends was killed by her partner, and it haunts me. At their conference, I talked about facts we can't deny: that domestic abuse is more widespread than we admit, and too many of us act like bystanders, turning the other way, deciding not to get involved, which sends the message that it's not our problem.

Football has a lot of work to do when it comes to changing this culture that tolerates violence against women. I work in an environment where women are constantly being downplayed, and people don't even realize it. It's unconscious. The things that we say, the things that we do, send a message. The NFL sends a message that women don't matter with the way that, for years, it has ignored the issue of violence against women by players. The NFL also sends a message through how the league markets itself to the general public. We're stuck in a 1950s mind-set. The message is that a woman is only important as a cheerleader or, at most, a sideline reporter. We do this even though women make up almost half the NFL's fan base.

For a month we players dress in pink for breast cancer awareness, but we do nothing for awareness about sexism or domestic violence. It's as if the sexism baked into the league is more important than the financial benefits that could be gained by treating our female fans with the respect they deserve. I need to do this work in the outside world, but I also need to push where I stand as well.

This is where my daughters come into the picture. Any struggle I take part in on their behalf is my way of paying them back for how they have changed my life. They have allowed me to evolve in a way that I think most football players never get to experience.

By the time most players are retired, they don't know how to talk to women like human beings. They don't know how to interact with their wives or girlfriends. That's why the divorce rate for retired NFL players is over 80 percent. I'm not against divorce. If a marriage isn't working, then it isn't working. But it should end because two people are growing apart, not because one half of a couple hasn't grown at all.

This problem starts early, as high school sports stars are taught to see girls and women as objects, the sexual rewards of being a star athlete. Parents, coaches, and schools often reinforce this, instead of working to change it. I think all male high school athletes should take part in what is called the Coaching Boys into Men program, which teaches young men how to interact constructively with the girls and women in their lives.

And when girls express an interest in football, rather than saying, "Make them the cheerleaders," maybe we can encourage them to play, and also start saying, "Let's teach them how to coach or become an executive or how to own a team."

My daughters have opened my eyes to the need to move from philanthropy to activism, but I also credit Angela Davis, once again, and her book *Women, Race, and Class*—an amazing intersectional work that ties together why women's liberation is liberation for all of us. Even if you disagree with her politics or her stances on issues, you cannot deny her overpowering intellect, her journey, and the persecution she has suffered. You can't deny that she sat in solitary confinement and stayed in shape by doing pushups on the concrete floor. You can't deny how far she was willing to go and how much she was willing to sacrifice. Angela Davis, to me, is a beautiful person and a caring soul. She also does Pilates, and those are no joke. I have got to get back to that myself.

There are a lot of people who have money. There are a lot of people who have fame. But there are very precious few people out there dedicating their lives to making change. I look up to people like Tamika Mallory and Linda Sarsour, two of the organizers of the Women's March. I look up to Patrisse Cullors and Alicia Garza, two of the women who started the Black Lives Matter movement. I look up to Malala Yousafzai, champion of girls' education and Nobel Prize winner; the women of the entertainment community on the front lines of the Time's Up movement; and especially the USA gymnasts who faced down their abuser in court, the "trusted" team doctor who had assaulted them over decades.

Angela Davis's story in particular speaks to me, because it's also the story of sisters, much like the sisters I'm raising. When Angela was in prison, her sister Fania Davis Jordan was the one going around the world, speaking. Fania Davis

Jordan built those rallies to "Free Angela." She was doing a lot of work, but not too many people know of Fania, because she was willing to do the thankless organizing behind the scenes to make sure that her sister was freed and their work would be seen through. Fania Davis Jordan went into the Oakland public schools, where Black kids were being suspended or expelled just for looking at a teacher wrong— real school-to-prison pipeline stuff—and helped change the approach, which almost eliminated suspensions in a bunch of schools and saved a lot of kids from juvenile prison. The number-one factor in whether an adult goes to prison is not race or economics but whether they were in prison as a juvenile, and Fania Davis Jordan has spared so many that fate.

I say it: this is the power of sisters. Then I look at my daughters and say, "Know your role models. Be there for each other and be there for the world."

ATHLETES FOR IMPACT

No one changes the world who isn't obsessed.

—Billie Jean King

There is a famous photo from June 4, 1967, of what is called the "Ali Summit." Muhammad Ali, Jim Brown, Bill Russell, Lew Alcindor (soon to be Kareem Abdul-Jabbar), and several dozen other pro athletes stood together in solidarity with Ali for his resistance to the Vietnam War and refusal to submit his name for the draft. They also stated collectively that they believed that the stripping of Ali's heavyweight title, retaliation for his antiwar stance, was a grave injustice. It's a beautiful photo of a special moment. But it also makes me sad. I think about how important that solidarity was to Ali, for keeping him strong. And then I think about how different the world would be—both on and off the field—if they had been able to hold that organization of athletes from different sports together. Imagine if it had not only sustained itself but expanded over the past five decades.

Athletes in the last several years have done a lot of standing up and speaking out, whether in support of Black Lives Matter, Standing Rock, women's rights, or LGBTQ rights, and this is great. But we are also scattered and isolated. It's left us vulnerable and open to attack. I have been thinking a lot about the power of athletes, across the sports world, to join together for collective change. Kaepernick's protest, and what happened to him during the 2016 season, was the main inspiration for my desire to organize. Many of us around the league tried to come together to figure out how to support Colin. Different people wanted to do different things, but the message was the same: we have to act to relieve his burden. Sometimes groups of us texted each other with ideas or got together on group phone calls, but it always felt like a bunch of cooks in a kitchen who wanted to make the same dish but had different recipes. You can't organize that way. You need more than shared goals: you need shared plans and a shared organization to pound out those plans. It can't be "Just add water, make movement."

Imagine if we'd had an organization in place by 2016. We could have lifted a lot of pressure off of Colin's shoulders, called press conferences, held our version of the Ali Summit, and done something groundbreaking. We needed to bridge the gap between his individual heroism and an organization that can make sustained change. This isn't just true of Kaep. It's the lesson of the whole history of sports and politics. No one was there for Jack Johnson. No one was

there for Jackie Robinson. I think about Craig Hodges and
Mahmoud Abdul-Rauf, two NBA players who were forced
out of their league for being outspoken on injustice in the
1990s. No one in the NBA back then was willing to have
their backs. If there had been an organization rooted across
other sports, it could have helped Craig and Mahmoud keep
their jobs and even inspired the quiet NBA players of the
1990s to step up, too.

We need everyone on the playing field who is conscious to
come together in a single organization to support each other
when we speak out. We need to have each other's backs and
we need to be willing to act, together. So much value in our
society is placed on the individual. The "great man" myth is
a big part of our culture. Everyone is supposed to rise or fall
on their own hard work and achievement. But social change
requires solidarity, even—if not especially—in the world of
sports. When you look at history, any time our country has
moved in the direction of fairness and justice, a lot of people
acted together to make it happen.

I began talking with athletes and friends more than a year
ago about forming an organization—we thought we'd call it
"Athletes United." We allowed ourselves to imagine the size of
our collective platform. We don't all have 50 million Twitter
followers like LeBron, but together we could have 100 million. Shoot, if LeBron joined, we'd have 150 million. It would
be kind of like having our own union across different sports,
just for taking action on social issues. If there were this type of
umbrella for all athletes, no matter what sport they played or
league they were in, they would have a home for when things

get hot. We talked about forming a group that included some of the greatest male and female athletes willing to confront injustice. Not to put anyone on the spot, but I got excited thinking about an organization that brought together Colin Kaepernick and Megan Rapinoe; LeBron James and Breanna Stewart; the Williams sisters and the Bennett brothers, coming together to form the Super Friends of justice. Marshawn Lynch and Maya Moore; Chris Long and Justin Britt; Mario Balotelli and David Beckham. For real, David Beckham.

I think an organization like this could bring a lot of white athletes into the fold. We need more white players joining the struggle and stepping up. That's heroism, to me. Chris Long's public support of the anthem actions and his donations to scholarships that promote equality are heroism. We speak about Babe Ruth or Joe DiMaggio as being legends, and on the field, they were heroes. But there's nothing heroic about silence when human rights are being violated. White athletes are going to need some cover and support to really be a part of this, and a united group would be able to provide that.

Many players do important work with charitable foundations, providing after-school programs and sports camps for kids, helping the homeless, raising cancer awareness, and so much more. While this work is deeply needed, I have come to realize that we need to cross the bridge from philanthropy to activism. When Colin took a knee, it changed the national conversation about police violence and racism in a way that no amount of charitable giving could. Not everyone has been happy to have that conversation. Many even resent it, but these protests have reached people, especially white people, in a way that rivals the most powerful street demonstrations. The protests have been debated on sports radio, reaching an audience that has the luxury of not having to fear the police. After Trump attacked us, polls showed that even more people understood that the protests were about racism and police brutality, not about the president, free speech, or the flag. Even when others tried to co-opt it, our message came through, and I think that's because we were so disciplined. An organization could get out these messages even more effectively.

To outline my intentions, I drafted an opening declaration that read, in part:

> We, the undersigned people from the world of sports, are claiming our place at the front lines of the fight for a better world. There is too much oppression, too much pain, and too much hate throughout this country, and we can no longer afford to be silent.
>
> Athletes have a long history of being part of resistance movements. But often the athletes who speak out and take stands do so as individuals. Athletes United is an attempt to give an organizational expression to the voices for social justice in sports that have increasingly emerged over the last year. We can come together and support causes we care about vocally, organizationally, and financially, and in our numbers we will find an even greater strength.
>
> The need for such collective organizing is especially urgent right now. In a manner unprecedented for at least a generation, athletes from all sports and all walks of life have been speaking out. We have been speaking out against racism, sexism, and homophobia. We have been speaking

out against Trump's travel ban. We have been advocating for education, youth programs, and services to support the communities we come from. We have been speaking out on local community issues in ways that never make the media.

Especially now, faced with a president who is increasing the divisions in this country, we must not only speak out but act.

Little did I know that while I was making plans to launch Athletes United, an organization with a similar mission had formed. This team of organizers and athletes had seen the same potential and had already begun to lay the groundwork for collective action on a lot of important issues. They called themselves Athletes for Impact (A4I), and after speaking with them, I knew this would be my team off the field.

One of the first actions A4I took after I joined was to release a statement in support of Colin Kaepernick. It read, in part: "We call on all NFL owners, general managers, and coaches with a position to summon the courage to sign Colin Kaepernick and to stand with us on the right side of history. No one should be denied employment for having the courage to follow their convictions and take action for equality and social justice." Joining me in signing the letter were athletes including the All-Star center for the Phoenix Mercury, Brittney Griner, who won the 2012 ESPY Best Female Athlete Award; Olympic fencing medalist Ibtihaj Muhammad, the first US Olympian to compete wearing hijab; All-Star Seattle Storm forward Breanna Stewart, 2016 WNBA Rookie of the Year, who recently spoke bravely about sexual abuse she faced as a child; and legendary track and field Olympian John Carlos. We've begun planning an in-person meeting, where the athletes can come together to set the group's agenda and organizing priorities.

An organization like this is critical to moving athletes from being mad about things to actually doing something. Right now, when I talk to my teammates, a lot of them crave the idea of doing more, but they don't know the steps. They don't have a map to get them to a place where they are "doing something." That requires organization. I've described how pro athletes live in a bubble, where having a job is dependent on being focused from 6 a.m. to 6 p.m. every day. So, if they are going to do something outside that bubble, it needs to be simple, user-friendly, and all boxed up, ready to go. And that's exactly what can happen with A4I.

As A4I develops, we could meet once or twice a year, with a board or elected steering committee to set an agenda, and at these meetings the membership would have a say in the group's direction, like shareholders. Over time, the board members could change so younger athletes would always be part of the leadership—because they have their fingers on the pulse of the pros, yet they are also not so far away from the realities of the NCAA and high school sports life.

I also see travel as important, with the group setting up trips and programs in less fortunate countries. This could open the eyes of high school athletes who have never traveled outside the country, and it would be uncomfortable for those people who think leaving the country means chilling at the beach in the Bahamas. But the problems around the world are our problems, too, and I've seen with my own eyes the impact we could have with the most basic effort.

One thing I feel strongly about is that this organization needs to be, pardon the expression, for athletes and by athletes. Too often when an athlete gets an idea, everybody's well-meaning "team" gets in the way. Where there are managers and agents who understand our mission of social change as being more important than endorsement deals, we welcome their support. But the organization has to be for us and by us if it is going to be sustainable. Individuals burn out. Solid organizations last, and I think that somewhere along the way, as athletes, we have to be willing to ask ourselves, "What are we doing with the influence we have? Who do we need to be?"

But beyond the pros with the names, eventually I see this as involving any active athlete across the world. It starts with the pros, with the people who have influence, visibility, and some authority to speak out. Then we could open up our membership to NCAA athletes, hamstrung by their own situation. Higher-ups might think they could punish college athletes for joining a group like this, but let the NCAA just try to tell scholarship athletes that they have no right to take part in an organization on their own time. Let's see how well that goes over.

Once we had that base, we could talk seriously about reaching out to high school athletes, kids in middle school, elementary school. Whatever it takes. Imagine a high school soccer player who wants to figure out how to use her position and leadership as an athlete to raise awareness in her school about violence against women. We could connect her with speakers who are pro athletes, do workshops with different teams, connect her with local or legal organizations, hold forums in her city, and supply her with all of these resources right through her phone or laptop. We could also offer travel opportunities for young athletes to broaden their horizons about the issues that move them. This network of athletes can have a deep and intense influence on youth, giving them a voice and a platform. We can teach them that the aspiration is not to wear an NFL uniform but to change the world. Young people have tremendous passion inside them. We can cultivate their experiences to show them that they're not victims of their circumstances but the masters of them.

I have an after-school program in Houston I call Building Class. For forty-five minutes we talk to young people about how to be leaders, to build character and show them that they are the future. Instead of saying, "I'm Michael Bennett. Be like me," we say, "Okay, let's help you find out who you are and what you are passionate about." I see a united organization of athletes being able to multiply that kind of mentoring a thousand times. We can even link up athletes across the globe.

We have a long way to go, but I really feel that athletes are starting to wake up to the power they have, economically, culturally, and politically. When we fully realize it, what we can accomplish will be beyond everyone's wildest dreams. Imagine if all the athletes sponsored by Nike announced, "We're not going to wear any more of your products unless you put dollars into our inner-city schools that are falling apart, with old books and in poor condition, yet all the kids have on new kicks and are dying in fights over your products." You think they wouldn't give in to that demand? Did you see how quickly Under Armour changed its tune after Steph Curry, Misty Copeland, and The Rock—the company's most prominent endorsers—said they didn't like the CEO's statement supporting Trump? Athletes have so much untapped power, and once we realize what we can really do, the sky is the limit.

To help us get there, A4I has outlined a position statement on some of the issues that matter the most to us, including police violence, the economy, gun violence, LGBTQ equal rights, education, climate change, immigration, and mass imprisonment. Here is the Athlete Manifesto and Vision Statement that I helped draft:

Athlete Manifesto

As an athlete and leader with the opportunity to influence my local community, I recognize my responsibility to use my voice and resources to make a difference. I understand the critical role athletes can play as catalysts for social change. I am committed to supporting initiatives that bring people together and educate in ways that can actively transform our local neighborhoods and communities. As an Athlete for Impact and champion for change, I agree to the following #A4I principles.

As an Athlete for Impact, I will:

ADVOCATE for progressive change in my community and country through the use of my influence and platform;

COLLABORATE with organizations to create structural change by offering my assistance to local and national organizing efforts;

UNDERSTAND that the work I do doesn't stop with me and that justice issues are intersectional; and

PLEDGE to encourage my friends, family, fans, and fellow athletes to get involved in transforming America.

The Values

We, the undersigned people from the world of sports, are claiming our place at the front lines of the fight for a better world. There is too much oppression, too much pain, and too much hate throughout this country, and we can no longer afford to be silent.

Athletes for Impact believes that athletes should be celebrated for their work as activists and that all athletes can add value to social justice movements, no matter how many endorsements they have or how big their playing contract. Athletes for Impact believes:

In the right to speak in support of our core values and beliefs. Athletes are often told to be quiet and play the game and that activism has no place on the field of play. We refuse to relinquish our right to speech just because we play sports and will defend athletes who are being attacked because of their beliefs.

In inclusiveness, equity, and the inherent dignity of every single person, regardless of race, gender identity, class, abilities, sexual orientation, religion, or immigration status.

In the power of grassroots organizing as a way to empower local residents to come together, find solutions, and advance a more equitable future for all communities.

In voting and civic activism as a concrete way to address systemic and structural barriers to the overall health and well-being of our communities.

In economic justice and investment in young people and their families to enable them to be engines of social change and transformation.

In collaboration between athletes, grassroots organizers, advocacy organizations, governing bodies, and entities working on social and economic justice.

In internationalism. This not only an organization for athletes in the United States, and we affirm our commitment to stand up for our fellow athletes internationally as well as for human rights around the world.

I'd never thought that organizing with other athletes would be so important to me, but over the last several years, I've seen that many people in sports want to be a part of this conversation, but they're scared. The fear is rooted, when all is said and done, in a fear of retaliation, lost income, isolation, and even being killed. The fact that you can be persecuted for what you say is a scary thing. As LeBron said about Trump, "He made it fashionable to hate." Yes, there is a lot of hate out there. But there is such a contrast between speaking out as an individual and as a member of an organization. There is a critical connection between an organization and your ability to speak out safely. Yes, people will tell us to stick to sports. But, as Martellus drew in his cartoon, no one says, "Stick to sports" when you are using your spare time to sell McDonald's. Only when you try to effect change.

What I'm outlining could possibly be world changing: bringing together athletes from around the globe to build connections and movements through sports. I can already hear people saying it's impossible, but, as Nelson Mandela said, "Everything is impossible until you try." Mandela also said, "Sport has the power to change the world. It has the power to inspire. It has the power to unite people in a way that little else does. It speaks to youth in a language they understand. Sport can create hope where once there was only despair. It is more powerful than government in breaking down racial barriers." A lot of people cite that quote, but very few people have tried to put it into action, to test if the great man was right. We already know it doesn't pay to bet against Mandela. Now, I am going to help unite athletes in this cause and prove him right once again.

YOU HAVE TO FORGIVE TO GROW

Tennis is just a game, family is forever.

—**Serena Williams**

My birth mother, Caronda Bennett, is forty-eight years old. She made that decision to take my two younger siblings and leave Martellus and me with my father. Caronda was a seventeen-year-old girl with two children, a twenty-one-year-old with four children, and then a woman with five kids and a failing marriage. She chose not to raise Martellus and me.

And here she is, at my home, sitting around our dinner table with Pele and my three daughters. It's evening on Mother's Day 2017, one of those warm nights in Hawaii. The kind of evening where the breeze makes you feel open to the world.

I start dinner by saying grace and then I begin to cry. Six feet four, 275 pounds, and I am crying. I'm crying because I'm thinking about every moment growing up as a child, every moment we missed together, every moment I wanted to have *this moment*. My tears start falling and you could hear a pin drop in that kitchen. I explain to everyone—and it takes a moment for me to put it into words—that I'm not crying because I'm sad, I'm crying because I feel free of so much pain I didn't even realize was sitting on my chest.

I am attempting to bring Caronda back into our lives, and this dinner is a part of that. I could've said, "Forget her! She wasn't here for me." But I don't want to show my daughters that carrying pain, anger, and resentment is a way to live. How can I be the kind of father I want to be if I can't forgive? If I can't forgive my birth mother, how can I be out in the world arguing for love, justice, and community? How can I hold her hostage away from my heart for something she did when she was so young? My instincts are to stay angry, but my heart says that anger is the road to ruin.

I force myself to think about the cold truth: being a parent is challenging for me, and I'm thirty-one at this time, with all the resources I could ask for. She was a child, basically, just a few years older than my oldest daughter. At the time, she had more children than dollars in her pocket. I can't walk in her shoes, but I can guess that it probably felt, day in and day out, even worse than it sounds. So how can I not forgive her?

I know this is difficult for her, too. Remember, I'm thirty-one and she's forty-eight. We are practically peers. After grace,

I tell her I am proud to know her, and I say that I feel blessed just to be able to forgive her and build a relationship so we can finally care for each other. Then everyone starts crying. I am glad my daughters, young as they are, are here to see all this. I am glad we aren't hiding this from them. I want them to see all of this, and say to them that this is what a man looks like—a real man, not a façade. Not just a fearless person on the field. Not just someone who speaks at a rally. I don't want them to go their whole lives and say they never saw their father cry.

When my birth mom and I were trying to reconnect, I knew my dad and my mom who raised me were nervous. They were scared that I would get hurt, and I think maybe they were scared that this could end with my loving them less. I could never love them less. But I couldn't go on and not be connected to the person who birthed me simply because of the decisions she made at the most difficult time of her life. I told my parents that I was trying to reconnect with her because that is how they raised me. They raised me to be the kind of man who could forgive. It's not the 1920s or the 1950s, when you were told not to be emotional, not to kiss your wife in public, not to cry in front of your daughters, and that showing charity or forgiveness was somehow a sign of weakness. This is a time when people are growing, and there is an understanding that we are more than just this flesh, right here. Spiritually, I need to forgive her to grow. I can't love my wife fully unless I love my birth mom properly.

As we've gotten to know each other all these years later, I'm finding out that she is a great person. Just as much as I've been hurt, she has been hurting, too. She has been in Louisiana all these years, not bonded to Martellus and me. Think about how hard that's been for her, living in that tight-knit community, as Martellus and I made our way through the NFL. Every day, people are asking her about us, these sons she has had no connection with. It must have been devastating for her, like having a wound poked, day in, day out. Like the Greek myth of Prometheus, chained to a rock, having an eagle eat her liver every day, only for it to grow back and be eaten again. A *Groundhog's Day* of suffering. But now she can say to them, with a smile, "I'm reconnecting with my family, especially with my grandchildren."

Martellus isn't quite there yet. He's trying. I'm pushing him more and more to be able to do it, and he will get there in his own time. I tell him, "You have to let this go, the anger. And if you don't, you won't be able to grow."

Martellus did invite her to his wedding, in 2017. I think that was a big step. Before his wedding day, he hadn't seen her in ten years. It was a special moment, and I'm proud of him. My brother looks up to me, so the fact that I've made this decision to reconnect with her means he will take it seriously. It's like when he sees me being an activist, moving forward, seeing my dedication. He has slowly transformed from being seen as a comedian into a real risk taker, someone who will put himself out there. His way is different from my way, but at the end of the day, I see him making the change. He has always been the same Martellus, but now he is the man who, in 2017, as his Patriots team went on that Super Bowl run, was raising his fist during the anthem and doing it with Belichick standing five feet away. After their win he didn't go to the White House and was loud and proud about why.

But it's funny how everything comes back to the beginning. We grew together through the shared hurt of our birth mother's rejection, then we grew even closer through college, football, and being roommates. And now, as grown men, we still depend on each other. We carry each other's burdens and shoulder each other's pain, and I wouldn't have it any other way. As long as I'm moving forward safely, he will continue to take these small steps. It's like, "If Michael's not getting hurt, then there must be a place for me to do the same."

For years, Caronda has wanted to have a relationship, and I cannot deny her that. I don't want my kids growing up and not knowing the full truth of who they are or who their family is. I take them to Louisiana to see Bennett Road so they can know a place where "everybody on the street is your family." I tell them, "This is where you started. Your ancestors, after slavery, this is where they settled. After they were freed, this is the land that they had. This is the church that everybody in your family went to and that your grandfather built with his bare hands. All these people on this street, they are some form of cousin." I think sometimes when my kids go back, they can't believe how much family they have.

I try to tell them that when I die, I want my funeral to be like Muhammad Ali's. He wasn't buried in Africa. He wasn't buried in Beverly Hills. He was buried in his hometown of Louisville. I think when you die, if you are truly at peace, you should return to the beginning, and Louisiana is the beginning for me. As much as we're removed from Bennett

Road and as much as I travel around the world, this is home. I wanted my birth mom in our lives to complete the puzzle for my children. I tell them, "Just as much as Miss Pennie is your grandma, Caronda is your grandma. They both are your grandmas, and that's okay. If somebody don't understand your story, they don't need to understand it. You have three grandmothers, and that's okay." That's life. I just wanted them to know that there is this lady who loves them: "She loves you, and you do exactly what she tells you to do simply because she's your grandma."

Now she stays with us for a week or two at a time. I've also taken her places she had never been before. She had never seen Florida. She had never been to Seattle. She had never seen the ocean, so I took her to see the ocean for the first time. To be her son and to be able to take her to different places, take her to eat food she's never experienced—it's been making up for a lot of lost time.

I don't think I could have opened up to this without support from Pele. It was so important for her to see me be able to move past the resentment. A lot of people might be like, "She hurt you already, just move on. Let's go to the beach." Instead, it was, "Your birth mom should come here. I'm booking a ticket for her now."

But that's how we have always rolled together. We bring the support for each other. There are times I need her to be strong, to say, "No, Michael, you're wrong. That's not the truth." Or, "Michael, you need to get beyond that."

When Pele set me on course, I knew I needed to forgive and try to bring the family together because, out of us five brothers and sisters, I'm the big brother. As the big brother, you lead your family. I tell my dad all the time: he's the father, so the family will always look up to him for certain things, but my brothers and sisters look up to me for a lot of things they would never talk to him about.

I feel like I have an even bigger responsibility with this family because of having two moms. I'm trying to keep the family together and help us grow, to push the envelope and develop together. I'm asking everyone, "How far can this family go? How much can we forgive? How much can we inspire each other to love each other more?" Some of them tell me they're exhausted by my efforts. They say, "I'm not built to forgive this much. I just want to live."

I tell them, "People make mistakes, and now they want to make amends. They can change, and you have to give them the chance to do that." My birth mother has evolved. You can't torture people with distance when they are trying to do right. This country has torn apart the Black family—the African family—in a thousand different ways. We cannot tear each other apart. That's a form of resistance we need to take seriously.

The next step, in my mind, is my mom and birth mother and dad, all sitting together around the table, forgiving one another in front of my daughters. I have told my dad that this is what I hope to see next, and who knows, maybe by the time you are reading this, it has already happened. That needs to be the next step for us to grow. Once the kids and grandkids see the elders forgive, the barrier will be broken and our family will flourish.

My dad will be the one who needs to shift. That man is like granite. He's old school, from a generation that still sees emotions as something you don't share, like an old-movie cowboy. I think he still carries pain about my birth mother all these years later. I think he never forgave her, and until he forgives her the wound won't heal. That will happen. I feel it in my heart, but I don't think he's there yet. Nothing against him, but it puts pressure on me to be the bridge between people and the glue to hold us together, to keep pushing the envelope, and to try to move everyone out of their comfort zones. This book is called *Things That Make White People Uncomfortable*, but forgiving your family? That is one thing that truly does transcend skin color. That's on all of us to confront. If it makes us uncomfortable, that's a sign we need to try harder.

As for my mom who raised me, Miss Pennie, she is a little scared, too. I don't think she'd ever admit it, but I think she carries some fear that our relationship could suffer. I want Miss Pennie to understand that she is my mom. She raised me. Everything that I am is because of her. Her gift of teaching me how to question the world is something I'll never be able to repay. I want her to know that no matter how much my relationship with my birth mom grows, it doesn't take anything away from our bond. It makes her an even greater mother, a greater human being, to have done what she did: taking on somebody else's children and raising them as her own. Her whole life is a testament to her character. There's more than enough place for both of my moms in my heart and around my table. That's my dream: a Mother's Day celebration, where all the mothers are together. We go around the table, my daughters, Pele, and then me, and we all say what our mother means to us—and I get to talk twice. That's my idea of peace.

The pain that I've felt on this journey of reconnecting with my birth mom is something I need to share. I want to share it so maybe someone who is experiencing something similar doesn't feel all alone in the world. I think when you feel isolated is when you do self-destructive things, like harm yourself or withdraw and become some kind of hermit. We share our stories so we feel less alone.

I can't separate the efforts to forgive and put my family together with my efforts to try and organize to change the world. Forgiveness has always been central to our Black freedom struggle. I mentioned this to my dad to try to help him along on this road. I said, "Think about Dr. Martin Luther King. He literally could walk into a room and be spit on, kicked, hit with a brick, have lit cigarettes flicked at his face, and keep walking, keep a level head, and show love. He was literally walking and forgiving people as they committed these transgressions because he knew to get to where he wanted, spiritually, he had to do it."

I don't know if I can ever reach that level. I still get mad when a coach yells at me or some member of the media asks me a dumb question. (Five minutes after losing a game: "So, how do you feel about that loss?" How do you think I feel? Even Dr. King might smack someone for asking something that dumb.) But I think that has to be the goal: the ability to forgive someone on the spot. It's so easy to throw a punch. It's so easy to shoot back. But to be able to forgive? There's an organization of the families of murder victims that protests against the death penalty. That's the level we need to aspire to. It's not easy when revenge is held up in movies and music as the ultimate expression of manhood, instead of how it should be seen: as the response of the child.

I would argue that to get to that level of mercy and grace starts at home. It starts with forgiving people. I told that to my dad, and he was silent. Then he said, like that old-movie cowboy, "I never even thought about that." It was small, but I felt him move in my direction, toward where I hope he can go.

In each case, the need to forgive has to happen before you can achieve justice. I can forgive anyone for anything they have said or done, or that their ancestors said or did, as long as they are willing to work with me to make sure today's version of Jim Crow—from mass imprisonment to inferior access to education and nutrition, to police violence—gets beaten back. There is a need to forgive but never forget, because if we are not honest about the past, we will never change our present or future. If it makes some people uncomfortable, then that's the price of change. It's not comfortable to confront the part of our history that make us feel shame. It's not comfortable for me to sit for the anthem while people boo. It's not comfortable to lose sponsors or give away endorsements. It's not comfortable to go to parts of the world or parts of this country where suffering is a way of life. But guess what? You have to be uncomfortable to grow. When you grow as a child, it's so intense that your body is knocking your own teeth out of your mouth so stronger, better teeth can grow in. When your bones are growing when you're twelve, thirteen years old, it can be so uncomfortable you can't sleep at night. If we feel uncomfortable, we are doing something right. That discomfort is just a period of transition.

It's not comfortable to see people in Flint, Michigan, without clean water. It's not comfortable to hear gymnasts tell their stories of being sexually assaulted. It's not comfortable to talk about CTE. It's not comfortable seeing kids too tired to move. But the ultimate question is: *What are you going to do? Are you going to lay it on the line? Are you going to be a change-maker?* Remember what John Carlos said: "There is no partial commitment to justice. You are either in or you're out." Trust me: if you're willing to be uncomfortable, you will also feel blessed, if you can see it through and make it to the other side.

AFTERWORD: GET COMFORTABLE

I was out with the kids, and we met a dude on the beach. He was a Latino guy from Portland, and he was flying a kite. He saw me with my daughters and asked, "You guys like kites?"

I asked him, "How much did that kite cost?"

He said, "Oh, about ten dollars from Costco."

I said, "I wanna get a kite."

He replied, "Hold on. I have two kites. Take one. But first, let me show you how to fly mine."

He demonstrated how to do it. Then I let my daughters take turns, but we ended up tangling it all up. It was a mess. Most people would have said, "I let you use my kite and you tangled it up. What is your problem?"

Instead, he just smiled and told me, "You know what, I got kids too. Kids can mess stuff up, but it's about the experience, man, and it's cool that your kids got to play with the kite. It's just part of learning, brother."

I was like, "Man, take my number. If you're ever on the other side of town, call me."

He didn't know I played in the NFL or nothing. When I asked him, he didn't know a Seahawk from a mountain lion. He was just a cool person, and that's the kind of people you meet along the way in life. There's a whole bunch of great people out there, and when you let yourself be vulnerable, not build walls between yourself and others, you can make change. You have to open yourself up and get comfortable with your discomfort. Then you don't need to build more walls. Instead, they just come tumbling down.

ABOUT HAYMARKET BOOKS

Haymarket Books is a radical, independent, nonprofit book publisher based in Chicago. Our mission is to publish books that contribute to struggles for social and economic justice. We strive to make our books a vibrant and organic part of social movements and the education and development of a critical, engaged, international left.

We take inspiration and courage from our namesakes, the Haymarket martyrs, who gave their lives fighting for a better world. Their 1886 struggle for the eight-hour day—which gave us May Day, the international workers' holiday—reminds workers around the world that ordinary people can organize and struggle for their own liberation. These struggles continue today across the globe—struggles against oppression, exploitation, poverty, and war.

Since our founding in 2001, Haymarket Books has published more than five hundred titles. Radically independent, we seek to drive a wedge into the risk-averse world of corporate book publishing. Our authors include Noam Chomsky, Arundhati Roy, Rebecca Solnit, Angela Davis, Howard Zinn, Amy Goodman, Wallace Shawn, Mike

Davis, Winona LaDuke, Ilan Pappé, Richard Wolff, Dave Zirin, Keeanga-Yamahtta Taylor, Nick Turse, Dahr Jamail, David Barsamian, Elizabeth Laird, Amira Hass, Mark Steel, Avi Lewis, Naomi Klein, and Neil Davidson. We are also the trade publishers of the acclaimed Historical Materialism Book Series and of Dispatch Books.

Also available from Haymarket Books

Brazil's Dance with the Devil: The World Cup, the Olympics, and the Struggle for Democracy
Dave Zirin

From #BlackLivesMatter to Black Liberation
Keeanga-Yamahtta Taylor

The John Carlos Story: The Sports Moment That Changed the World
John Wesley Carlos and Dave Zirin,
foreword by Cornel West

Long Shot: The Triumphs and Struggles of an NBA Freedom Fighter
Rory Fanning and Craig Hodges,
foreword by Dave Zirin

What's My Name, Fool?: Sports and Resistance in the United States
Dave Zirin

ABOUT THE AUTHORS

Michael Bennett is a three-time Pro Bowler, Pro Bowl MVP, Super Bowl Champion, and two-time NFC Champion. He has gained international recognition for his public support for the Black Lives Matter movement, women's rights, and other social justice causes. In 2017, he was named one of the 100 Most Influential African Americans by the *Root*, was the Seattle Seahawks nominee for the NFL's Walter Payton Man of the Year award, and was honored, along with his brother Martellus, with a BET Shine a Light award for exceptional service.

He is the cofounder with Pele Bennett of The Bennett Foundation, which educates underserved children and communities through free, accessible programming. He has held free camps and health clinics in Seattle, in his hometown of Houston, in his current off-season home of Honolulu, and in South Dakota with the Lower Brule Sioux Tribe.

He donates all of his endorsement money and the proceeds from his jersey sales to fund health and education projects for poor and underserved youth and minority communities, and he recently expanded his reach globally to support STEM programming in Africa.

He is the proud father of three daughters, Peyton, Blake, and Ollie.

Dave Zirin is the sports editor for the *Nation* and the author of several books, most recently *Jim Brown: Last Man Standing*. Zirin is a frequent guest on MSNBC, ESPN, and *Democracy Now!* He hosts WPFW's *The Collision* with Etan Thomas and the *Edge of Sports* podcast.

Martellus Bennett is the younger brother of Michael Bennett. When he's not singing Michael's praises, he's creating awesomeness at his multimedia company, The Imagination Agency, and making the NFL more fun.